Building Natural
Stone Garden Features

Building Natural Stone Garden Features

ANDY RADFORD

THE CROWOOD PRESS

First published in 2007 by
The Crowood Press Ltd
Ramsbury, Marlborough
Wiltshire SN8 2HR

www.crowood.com

British Library Cataloguing-in-Publication Data
A catalogue record for this book is available from the British
Library.

ISBN 978 1 86126 954 6

Dedication
This book is dedicated to Janet Williams, my partner.

Acknowledgements
I would like to thank the following individuals for their invaluable
help with producing this book: Ruth Woodcock, whose garden is
featured as the book's main project; Alan Leighton, who assisted
me with the construction work; Aron Walsh, who also assisted with
some of the book's projects; John Barlow who kindly loaned power
tools free of charge. A special thank you to Tony McCormack from
www.pavingexpert.com, who kindly supplied the information
regarding natural stone suppliers within Great Britain.

Typeset by Carreg Limited, Ross-on-Wye, Herefordshire

Printed and bound in Singapore by Craft Print International

Contents

Introduction

The majority of people reside in urban or metropolitan areas where the chance to experience the beauty of natural stone is severely limited. Many of today's new structures in cities and towns are constructed using modern materials, but older buildings such as churches and some municipal facilities still proudly show off skilled, dressed faces of natural stone. One could be forgiven for thinking that a dry stone wall or a garden hosting natural stone features would appear lost and out of place in these districts. This may be true, but as part of a traditional garden theme natural stone comes into its own, be it in a city centre or perched on the side of a mountain, surrounding some sleepy, ancient cottage.

As a professional landscape gardener, my personal feelings toward the shape and feel of a garden are biased on the side of the countryside. After all, isn't this the ultimate purpose behind a garden? A miniature fragment of the rolling hills and shaded woodland within easy reach of our back doors, a secure space in which one may unwind and lift the stresses of everyday life, if only for a fleeting, special moment. A garden, to all intents and purposes, is our own private shred of customized countryside, indulging our individual needs and desires, specifically designed to create the peace and freedom only nature can offer.

A relaxing garden is one that can transport you to the serenity of a mountainous lakeland, adorned with sylvan and floral architecture, a place where the elements of nature entwine to form a myriad of special, private moments. Unfortunately a grandiose theme such as this can only be achieved if you are lucky enough to own a Scottish island or an entire mountain range, but the symbolism of this paradise can easily be transposed to fashion any garden plot, large and small, city centre or otherwise.

UNDERSTANDING NATURAL STONE

The varied appearance and styles of stone construction are down to the inherent differ-

The author – Andy Radford.

ences in the availability and properties of the locally found stone.

Different Types of Rock

The landscape of Great Britain is incredibly varied, often changing completely within a few miles. The reason for these dramatic transformations lies beneath the surface of the soil, in the large number of different types of bedrock. Individual rock types have varying properties, which leads to different patterns of erosion. This island has seen massive geological upheaval in the distant past, leading to rock types of different age and constituents surfacing side by side despite being formed millions of years apart. It is difficult to believe, looking at the rolling hills and valleys of today, that it was violent volcanic activity and land movements that led to their formation.

There are three rock types: igneous, sedimentary and metamorphic. Igneous rocks, such as granite, are formed when hot molten rock cools down and solidifies. They appear in two forms, intrusive and extrusive. Intrusive rocks cool below the surface and extrusive rock cools above ground. As they tend to be crystalline, igneous rocks are very hard and difficult to break, and form areas of high ground. Whilst this property makes the stone resistant to erosion, it has the disadvantage of making it very difficult to dress to shape using walling tools.

Sedimentary rock is formed when particles of material are laid down and subsequently compressed. The particles might be a result of erosion of pre-existing rock, or they might be organic matter such as shells or animal bones. There are many differing rocks of this type, but the two examples that are widely used by dry stone wallers and stone masons are sandstone and limestone. Sandstone arises from compressed sand particles and shale, but was originally derived from compressed mud. Limestone is made from the bodies of sea creatures and is predominantly calcium carbonate. Chalk is also predominantly calcium carbonate, but is a much softer rock than

limestone. Sedimentary rock is laid down in bedding planes, and is easy to split along these planes. Whilst this leads to the rock being less resistant to erosion, it makes it ideal for the landscape gardener to dress and use. Also stone of this type tends to have good 'faces', which again makes it ideal for stone features.

Metamorphic rock is formed when existing rock (either sedimentary or igneous) is subjected to immense heat or pressure, or a combination of both. These conditions could have occurred at times when volcanic activity or earth movements were prevalent. Since most types of metamorphosed rock tend to be valuable – such as marble – they are not likely to be used for building. However, one type of metamorphic rock is extremely common in Great Britain and that is slate. Slate was formed when shale was subjected to volcanic activity, and is prevalent in upland areas, particularly in Wales, Cornwall and parts of the Lake District. Slate is easy to use for walling and has been used extensively in Snowdonia. Its useful properties include cleavage: it is easy for a skilled person to break slate along the original bedding planes of the shale.

Erosion

All three rock types are subject to erosion, which can be chemical or mechanical. Chemical erosion occurs when the actual constituents of the rock are dissolved by acid; this is called 'chemical weathering'. Weathering takes place when carbon dioxide in the air combines with rainwater and falls to earth as acid rain, which in turn penetrates the surface of the stone. All rock types are susceptible to this action, though the harder rocks such as granite take millions of years to be eroded in this way. If acidic minerals are present the process can be speeded up. Limestone and chalk have become more vulnerable since the advent of pollution.

Mechanical erosion occurs when natural variation in temperature causes the rock to expand and contract. This action results in large pieces breaking free from the main structure. The process is exacerbated when water penetrates along natural fault lines and then freezes. Eventually this results in piles of boulders being formed in exposed rocky areas, which would have been one of the original sources of material for upland farmers to use for construction. Other sources of building stone include quarries specifically excavated for enclosure purposes, and river beds.

Regional Variations

Many of the contrasts in styles of walling throughout the British Isles arise from differences in the properties and availability of local rock. As outlined earlier, there are many different bedrock types, all of which are millions of years old. An interesting thought for today's wallers and stone masons, when they pick up a stone to add it to a new structure, is that the material could have been formed even before the dinosaurs roamed the Earth.

The oldest rocks are the Pre-Cambrian, which form some of the ancient sandstones of upland Wales and southern Scotland. The bedrock in these regions was formed 3,400 million years ago, before life began. Later volcanic activity pushed up mountain ranges and created igneous and metamorphic rocks; this included regions of granite in Dartmoor and the Lake District. The mountains in these regions are made of very hard rocks that have resisted erosion. Large slabs of granite were used to build a dry stone drover's bridge on Dartmoor that is still in use today as a footbridge. At Grimspound, also on Dartmoor, there is a Bronze Age settlement that is completely surrounded by a dry stone wall made of granite.

Following this period of upheaval, these islands became a desert. During this period the old red sandstones were formed. This excellent building stone is predominant in Devon (hence the name Devon Red sandstone), and forms a band up the west of Britain through the West Midlands,

Shrewsbury and Chester up to the northwest of Cumbria. In the Dark Peak area of the Peak District National Park a similar type of stone is present, known locally as gritstone. In areas where this stone was present close to the surface there are ample examples of ancient dry stone structures made from this distinctive material. Sandstone, no matter in what form it presents itself, is easy to dress to size and shape, hence the beautiful, smooth faces usually seen on this style of wall.

During the Carboniferous period (between 345 million and 320 million years ago) Britain was covered with warm seas. During this period limestone was formed by the compression of the remains of sea creatures. The presence of Carboniferous limestone in this country has led to the formation of the distinctive landscapes of the Yorkshire Dales and the White Peak in the Peak District National Park. In these upland areas the construction of dry stone walls came into its own. The abundance of exposed areas of rock and the availability of piles of stone provided the ideal material for the hill farmers to construct stock-proof barriers. One of the great delights of building with this type of limestone is the presence of fossils. If the waller is not careful, it is possible to spend more time painstakingly chipping away with the walling hammer to extract specimens, than on the job in hand!

A different type of limestone was formed later, during the Jurassic period (around 195 million years ago). This limestone forms a ridge from Dorset through to the Cotswolds, and there is second ridge that finishes in the North York Moors. In the Cotswolds there are many fine examples of dry stone walls constructed from this limestone. Jurassic limestone is harder than the Carboniferous limestone, and is not so easy to wall with, mainly due to its small size and the lack of ideal stone to tie the walls together. It is for this reason that walls in the Cotswolds are lower in height than any other region.

Chalk is a very soft rock. It is present in southern England and forms the bedrock of the North and South Downs. There is also an area of chalk in the east, this is the bedrock that resulted in the formation of the Yorkshire Wolds. Chalk contains bands of fossilized remains resulting in bands of darker flints. Although chalk has not been used extensively to form dry stone walls as stock barriers, ancient tribes used it to construct buildings. Some of these structures remain today, evidence of the durability of this construction method.

The newest type of rock in the British Isles was formed during a second period of volcanic activity as recently as one million years ago. During this period the granites of the north of Scotland were formed. Dolerite was also formed in West Wales, this being the material used to build Stonehenge. There are examples of dry stone buildings made from this material in West Wales.

The origins of the stone craft are firmly rooted in the past, reaching back to a time before life, as we know it, began. The styles, shapes and appearances of stone walls are intertwined with the landscape and heritage of an area in a way that no other man-made structure ever can. The practitioner of this ancient art can be assured that, as he or she places each stone on to a wall, the act entwines a piece of history into a natural landscape, a human touch in complete harmony with nature, enhancing the appearance and conservation value of the countryside. There are not many building techniques in use today that have these kind of advantages!

CHAPTER ONE

Getting Started

HEALTH AND SAFETY

Working with Stone

As with all manual tasks that involve the handling of large construction materials, personal safety is of paramount importance in stonework. One must consider the fact that most lumps of building stone are very heavy and can cause severe injury if your concentration wanes or the fatigue of a day's work begins to settle in. You could be limping into the local casualty department dragging a broken foot, favouring a broken hand or bent forward with a strained back, and this could be before the job even gets underway. Physical fitness is a vital attribute, as the majority of stone constructions demand at least a day's labour. The project garden for this book spanned two working weeks of continual lifting and placing stone, and not an hour went by without having to haul rocks and place them carefully onto their specified place, and some stone even required the help of two people. So, one must really consider one's own personal fitness and health before embarking on a heavy project such as this.

There are many hidden dangers associated with different styles of stone. Slate and limestone, for example, can be razor sharp; sandstone is very abrasive to the hands and fingers; and all stone, when hit with a hammer, has the tendency to produce shrapnel-like projectiles that can fly toward unprotected eyes. Weathered slate, where the layers of rock are beginning to crumble or break away, can produce injuries similar to glass splinters. The main problem with slate, however, is that it tends to be dusty or encrusted with layers of dirt. Considering the fact that some natural stone might have spent part of its life in an agricultural environment, the prevention of tetanus infection ought to be of foremost importance.

Tetanus

Tetanus – also known as lockjaw – is a condition that affects the nervous system and causes painful, uncontrolled muscle spasms. Because of widespread immunization, tetanus is now rare. The disease is caused by a toxin produced by spores of the bacterium *Clostridium tetani*. Spores are hardy forms of the bacteria that can survive in the environment in an inactive state for a long time. Tetanus spores can be found throughout the environment, usually in soil, dust and animal waste, and can enter the body through a wound that is contaminated with material. Spores can get into the body through even a tiny pinprick or scratch, but they usually enter through deep puncture wounds or cuts. Tetanus spores can also enter the body via an existing injury. Once the spores enter a wound, they produce a powerful nerve poison that spreads quickly and causes painful symptoms.

The first signs of tetanus infection are usually a headache and spasms or cramping of the jaw muscles (lockjaw). As the poison spreads, it progressively attacks more groups of muscles, causing spasms in the neck, arms, legs and stomach, and sometimes violent convulsions. The time between the contamination of a wound and the first symptoms is usually less than two weeks, but it can range from two days to months. However, the shorter the time between exposure and symptoms, the more severe the disease. Tetanus is an easily preventable disease and it is advisable one consults a doctor for an immunization programme before any outdoors work commences.

Leptospyrosis (Weil's Disease)
Tetanus isn't the only potentially fatal disease associated with outdoors work. Leptospyrosis (Weil's Disease) is another common danger, especially around old ponds and waterways. Incidences of Weil's disease have been increasingly reported in people who work in the outdoors. You are at particular risk working in ponds and old drainage gullies. The disease is carried by rats and spread through their urine. Humans can contract it, through open wounds and abrasions whilst working in contaminated water. The first signs of infection are influenza-like symptoms. If this occurs, soon after a drainage or pond clearance task, immediate consultation with a doctor is required. If a blood test confirms the illness, quick treatment is required.

TOOLS OF THE TRADE AND SAFETY

As with all stone work, the most important tools you will need are your hands and a level head. The following is a list of essential tools, along with some alternatives that may be hanging up in the average garden shed:

Walling hammer This tool is similar to a lump hammer, and is designed for breaking and dressing stone. Walling hammers come in differing sizes and weights, but they all have a blunt end for breaking stone and a chisel end for cutting and shaping.

Lump hammer Can be used instead of a walling hammer.

Bolster chisel Used in conjunction with a lump or walling hammer, this is an ideal tool for cutting large stones to size.

Sledgehammer Used for breaking big stones.

Spade For digging out foundations and clearing debris.

Mattock or pick Mattocks and picks are ideal for breaking up small tree roots and loosening hard ground.

Crowbar A crowbar is shaped like a spear and is made out of strong metal. One end of the bar is pointed and therefore ideal for breaking up compacted ground. The other end of the bar is chisel-shaped and mainly used for splitting awkward stone within a foundation trench. Crowbars can be used also for moving fairly large pieces of rock around a work site.

Rake Used for dragging and levelling soil.

Bucket Handy for collecting hearting stone.

Wheelbarrow For moving quantities of stone and soil around the walling area. Wheelbarrows can be used for transporting sand and cement around the worksite.

Nylon string line Used for creating straight-faced edges.

Line level A line level is a small spirit level, designed to hang on a string. Setting up the string-lines with this inexpensive tool allows for very accurate placing of face-stones. This results in a highly aesthetically pleasing finished product.

Checking Your Tools
Before tools are used, they should be checked for their ability to do the job safely. A loose

hammerhead may slip from the shaft, caus-ing injury to oneself or another. Loose-fitting pick and mattock heads have the tendency to slide down the stale, causing potential injury to the user. If the shafts are rotten, replace them. If they have shrunk, which is some-times the case, a long soak in a bucket of water will help to swell the wood to the metal. When tools are not in use they should be stored in a safe place, away from access points or a child's play area, but preferably near the worksite.

Working with Walling Tools

- Do not swing mattocks, picks, sledge ham-mers and walling hammers above head height. This could unbalance the user when working on a hillside or cause injury to someone behind.
- Warn others before breaking stone.
- It is a good idea not to leave unused tools standing upright in case someone walks into them. Push the prongs of rakes into the ground. Find a safe storage area away from any paths and use it all the time. This way you'll know where the tools are and won't be wandering around in a daze won-dering where you last had the walling hammer or chisel.
- Wear eye protectors when breaking stone.

Mechanical Tools

There are many electrical and petrol-driven tools that make construction easier. The most obvious is a cement mixer, as it takes away the burden of mixing sand and cement by hand. Another handy tool is a petrol-powered stonecutter (often called a Stihl saw). Stihl saws are very similar to chainsaws in appear-ance, except that a diamond or tungsten cir-cular blade and guard replaces the chain-saw's bar and chain. I did not actually use a petrol stonecutter for this book's project gar-den for two reasons. Firstly, I wanted to con-struct the features using as much of the nat-ural stone shape as possible. Secondly, I felt it prudent to keep the use of specialist tools to

a minimum, considering that lay people might be following the techniques herein: these tools should really be operated by qual-ified people, wearing dust and eye protectors. If you *are* going to use a stonecutter, relevant safety information follows. I stress, however, that I do not advocate the use of this tool if one is not wholly familiar with it, and quali-fied to use it.

Stonecutter Safety
These power tools are operated by hand and pose varied risks to many parts of the body. Dangers associated with petrol stonecutters are: flying debris, sparks that could cause a fire, noise and dust pollution. Foot, hand, head, eye and hearing protection should be worn at all times when the tool is in use or rotating. The cutting disc revolves very fast, and it can sever fingers or cause deep wounds to other parts of the body. A stonecutter isn't a lightweight tool, it is in fact a fairly heavy, cumbersome machine and, like a chainsaw, can produce what is know as 'kick back'. This is when the tip of a tool glances on something and ricochets toward the user. This can occur at any time, more so when the tool operator is fatigued.

One very common injury associated with stonecutters is known as 'white knuckle'. This is caused by long exposure to the vibra-tion from the tool. Most stonecutters are fit-ted with an anti-vibration hand grip, but con-stant use without adequate hand protection is not advisable: a pair of anti-vibration/impact gloves should be worn. Information on safety clothing can found on the Health and Safety Executive's website (listed in the Useful Contacts at the back of this book).

Using Cement Mixers
Cement mixers, whether they are powered by electricity or petrol, represent a hazard if not used correctly. On machines with electric motors, check for frayed or broken cables. The machine must be plugged into a wall-mount-ed circuit breaker or one incorporated into an

extension cable. The cable should not run anywhere near the mortar tipping area, and should always be so laid to minimize the risk of anyone tripping over it. Petrol-driven machines should be checked for fuel leaks and not used if one is detected. To minimize spills when filling the fuel tank, always use a suitably sized funnel to avoid splashing, especially if the mixer has been running and the engine is still hot. Needless to say, do not smoke whilst handling fuel.

Both styles of mixer should be used on the recommended stands and placed on firm, flat ground and away from paths and walkways. To avoid cement damage to existing patios and garden features, use a tarpaulin or some other form of protective covering. When tipping the mixed mortar out of the drum, ensure it falls onto a large board or directly into a wheelbarrow.

The operational technique for mixers is exactly the same for both styles. Always make sure the cement mixer is switched on and the drum is revolving before loading sand, cement and water. When filling the drum with the mixing ingredients, stand to one side of the machine, ensuring the shovel does not enter and get caught up on the internal blades. Do not overfill the mixer: always check the operating manual for the correct ratios or consult the hire company. Before adding water, make sure the sand and cement has been correctly mixed together; you can tell this from the uniform colour of the mixture. Add small amounts of water until the mixture is not too wet and runny and not too dry and crumbly. If weather conditions are very hot, as it was whilst building this book's project garden, extra water should be added to counter quick evaporation. In winter, when there is a risk of overnight frost, the application of a builder's antifreeze solution with plasticizer is advisable. This has two benefits: it makes the mortar more pliable to lay and point, and it will protect the water molecules in the drying mixture from icing, which would render the mortar useless.

MORTAR AND RATIOS

Class II mortars are used for most applications. These include load-bearing constructions such as retaining structures, garden walls and other walls exposed to possible severe dampness. Mortar must not be used when it is beginning to set, which usually occurs about two hours after it has been mixed. If you are working on your own it is a good idea to mix small batches as they are required. Discard mortar that has stiffened so much that it is impossible to restore workability without adding more water. Sand and cement ratios will differ according to the job in hand – refer to the table below.

To make	Cement	Sand
Strong and most durable mortar mix for all wall constructions	1 unit	4 units
Reasonably durable mortar mix for patio construction	1 unit	5 units
Mixing for pointing	1 unit	4 units

SOURCING STONE

Quarries near areas of abundant, dry stone walling country usually cater for the specialist craftsman. Before contacting them work out the quantities you'll need: around 1 ton per metre of wall built to a height of 4ft 6in (1.4m). This will be enough to provide for pinning, hearting, throughs, face-stones, end stones and coping. The cost (in 2007) varies from as little as £30 per ton to as much as £120 per ton, depending on the type of stone required; this does not include VAT. Even if only a small quantity of stone is required, the cost of a 10-ton or 5-ton lorry will be added to the bill in the form of a delivery charge.

The type of available stone largely depends on where you live. If you reside in a

National Park or an Area of Outstanding Natural Beauty (AONB) you will have to use whatever material is in keeping with the locality.

Another good source is the local papers. In the small ads there are often adverts from individuals selling rockery stone – it could be a bargain or you may be expected to pay an extortionate price. Theft of stone is very common, so it is advisable to make sure the material you are about to purchase is from a legitimate source. On occasions, within the private adverts, I have found a person only too willing for the stone to be taken off their hands for nothing. This does come at price though: you will have to arrange collection and delivery yourself. If the project requires more than 1 ton it could mean a hefty fuel bill and the possible purchase or hire of a pickup or double-axle trailer.

As regards stone, the majority of builders' merchants deal only in pre-cast bricks and aggregates. Garden centres concentrate mainly on ornamental stone features, but a clued-up assistant or manager could point you in the right direction. You could even try popping down to the local Farmers' Union store or DIY outlet and glance over the private advertising boards. The stone is out there somewhere, and if you really want it you'll find it. There is an extensive list of UK quarries and stone suppliers at that back of this book. This information will be useful to people who reside in lowland regions where the use of natural stone is the exception rather than the rule.

CHAPTER TWO

Trimming and Cutting Stone

Tools

- Walling hammer or lump hammer and bolster chisel. In any case a bolster chisel should be part of your tool supply.
- Sledgehammer.
- Tape measure.
- Safety goggles. These must be worn at all times when breaking stone.

Method

At some stage, during the majority of stone tasks, lumps of material will have to be cut, trimmed or shaped to fit awkward gaps, regardless of the project in hand, whether it is building a wall, pond, crazy paved patio or certain styles of path surface. Most stone can be split or broken with a lump hammer and bolster chisel or with a walling hammer. Some varieties of stone lend themselves to trouble-free, accurate cutting, whilst others can only be roughly and haphazardly trimmed or broken. Regardless of the stone in use, all material must be manipulated on soft ground and not on the surface of a project area. The latter is particularly important when building dry stone walling courses or laying a crazy-paved area. Although it may appear safe to hold material by hand when gently chipping away at its edges, it is a dangerous practice, especially when breaking heavy walling matter. Large lumps of rock could fall to the ground and graze a shin, or bruise or break a foot.

Big stone is better supported against another stone and anchored firmly with a foot. Before breaking large stone, make sure it won't be needed as a through, coping stone, path surface material or edging.

Sandstone and slate

Sandstone and slate are the easiest materials to trim and shape with a walling hammer or lump hammer and bolster chisel. They are soft rocks, mostly built up with layers of sand and, in some cases, quartz and sand. The sandstone found in the Dark Peak area of the Peak District National Park, Derbyshire, is so soft, crumbly and effortless to shape that it's often referred to as 'sugar stone'.

If you have to shape sandstone to fit a certain shaped crevice, choose material that roughly resembles the character of the hole. Place the rock against the gap and with the bolster chisel, or some other type of scribing tool, roughly draw the outline on the stone. Laying the material on soft ground, take the walling hammer (or lump hammer and bolster chisel) and gently chip away within 0.5in (12mm) of the edges until the required form has been sculpted.

A situation might arise when a certain thickness of stone will be wanted to raise the level of a dry stone walling course. If this is the case then the material can be split down the 'bedding plane' (discussed in the Introduction). There are two planes to consider

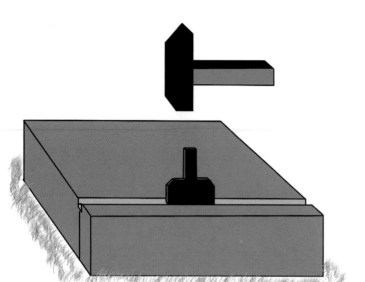

Chiselling the groove.

here, the other one being the 'cleavage plane'. The cleavage plane (or cleavage) can be found on certain metamorphic rock types, often running at an angle from the bedding plane. Stone should be split whilst being supported vertically. On sandstone, bedding planes can be recognized by the different-coloured lines running through the stone. It is here where the stone should be split. The bedding planes on slate are often visible by the fact that these lines have already began to split due to frost damage. Using the bolster chisel and lump/walling hammer, apply medium force down the plane and you will soon see the material beginning to split as the chisel is forced further down.

This is where cleavage comes into play. When the chisel meets the cleavage plane, which runs across the bedding planes, the stone will split away at this point. This is fine

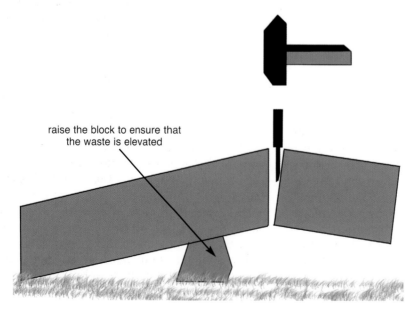

raise the block to ensure that the waste is elevated

Cutting the waste stone.

if what breaks away is an ideal size for the job in hand, but if you were looking for a longer item you will have to continue cutting down the bedding plane. On occasions, when the rock is too big, it may not split easily. Nevertheless, a crack will be formed that can be gently and slowly forced apart with light strikes of the hammer and chisel.

Breaking large sandstone to size, to create ideal throughs or path edges, involves a slightly different approach. Firstly, measure the section of wall or path you are working on, then transfer this length to the stone, ensuring that the material is on soft ground. Next, using the bolster chisel or a scribing tool, draw a cutting line across the top and down both sides. The stone must now be propped underneath; you can use smaller materials for this, but make sure the cutting line is proud of the supporting rock. Taking the lump/walling hammer and chisel, apply light to medium force to channel out the top and side cutting lines. As soon as this has been achieved, place the bolster chisel so it is the centre of the top line and then hit it with the hammer, applying firm force. The stone will now break away evenly from the channels. Breaking weathered slate in this manner is slightly less accurate and the edges may require further, gentle trimming with the walling hammer.

Limestone

Limestone poses interesting problems when it is trimmed or cut. Being a carboniferous rock, limestone does host bedding planes (or fissures) and, like sandstone and slate, it contains planes that run across the stone. These are called 'joints'. Limestone invariably contains fossils that make it difficult to cut accurately. In fact, trimming limestone to an ideal size is a hit and miss affair, as the vibration and energy of the hammer will often break the rock down a fissure that is nowhere near the area you are cutting. Weathered limestone is even harder to shape, because it is brittle due to years of water and frost damage. I don't bother cutting this type of rock if I am looking

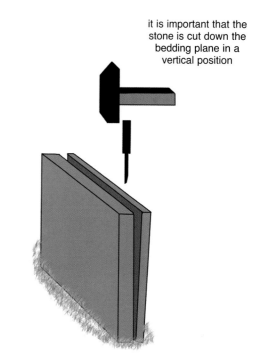

it is important that the stone is cut down the bedding plane in a vertical position

Cutting the stone along the bedding plane.

for a certain size: instead, I take my time searching for available materials around the worksite (obviously not from an existing wall) or, as a last resort, I smash larger pieces with a sledge hammer, by hitting the centre of the stone. If you have to this, you must be aware that this action produces missile-like shards that spread in all directions.

Granite

Granite is a very hard rock and almost impossible to cut and shape with normal tools. Owing to the time it takes to accurately shape this stone most dry stone wallers just make use of the available material as it comes. On the high granite regions in northern and south-western England and some parts of Scotland boundary walls are constructed with just a single course, predominately built using large, random, granite throughs. This was a technique that was developed because of the solid nature of the material; building a single-skin wall is a specialist walling task.

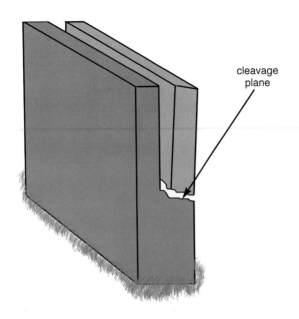

cleavage plane

Cleavage plane.

NATURAL STONE RAISED POND

The water feature project for this book is a raised, natural stone pond. I chose this construction for its aesthetic and safety features and because it is an unusual design. Raised ponds offer greater protection to children than a sunken, ground-level feature, as people do not tend to trip and fall into raised ponds. The construction techniques, including suitable pond liner materials, are discussed in Chapter 7. I have also added some information and construction advice on smaller water features such as pebble pools and an exciting but fairly large, child-safe, standing stone waterfall.

NATURAL STONE PATIO AND SEATING AREA

The project garden consisted of two patios, a small seating area constructed from awkwardly shaped random stone, mainly to show how effective these 'misshapes' – that otherwise might be ignored – can be. This is stone you might already have in your garden, or material that will be cheaper to purchase and easier to get hold of. The second patio is the larger of the two and was laid with material, hand picked for its shape and suitability from a quarry. The project patio and seating area were laid on a bed of mortar. A further technique for laying stone or flags on firm soil will also be discussed.

it is important that the stone is laid flat on the ground

weathered limestone is very difficult to cut accurately because of its brittle nature; when breaking strike firmly in the centre and wear eye protection

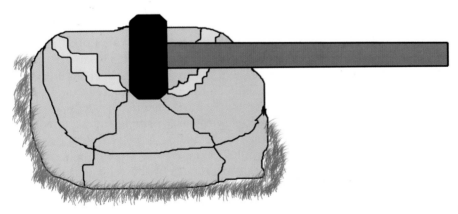

Breaking large stone.

SMALL HENGE AND STONE SEAT

Whilst considering the features for this book I wanted to bring something different to the reader. I could have constructed a barbecue or some other common ornament, but there are many books on the market that describe the building of these constructions. As the garden was on two levels, and the features were all stone, I decided to opt for a sympathetic symbiosis to enhance the natural raised areas of the ground, hence the pond I have just described. Ponds, however, are common and the two features I decided on were a stone circle or 'henge' and natural stone seat. These constructions are discussed in Chapter 8.

STONE STEPS

Even though a set of stone steps was an existing feature of the project garden, therefore not a construction feature of the book, I have none the less included the building method for wet and dry stone steps in Chapter 9.

RAISED STONE PLANTING BEDS

Although not part of the project garden, a project concerning raised beds for plant and vegetable growing is described in Chapter 8.

WALLING

Dry stone walls are becoming a very popular feature in many gardens. Not only are they a durable method of building a boundary, they are also aesthetically pleasing. The most common style of wall within the garden plot is the retaining wall, which is ideal for the creation of solid barriers and edges for raised borders. In a broader sense, the most important use of dry stone walls is as field boundary walls, commonly found in the upland regions of Britain. Chapter 10 describes the basic methods required to erect a retaining wall and free-standing boundary wall. There is also a brief description of the cemented version, but preference is given to dry stone construction, for the simple reason that they are cheaper to build and have a much longer life, if constructed and looked after correctly.

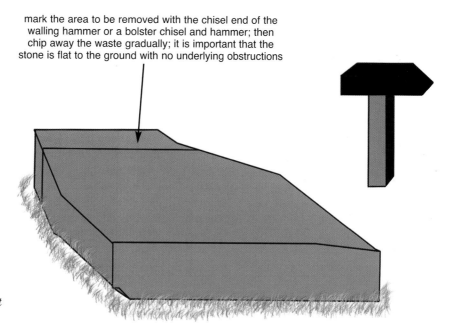

mark the area to be removed with the chisel end of the walling hammer or a bolster chisel and hammer; then chip away the waste gradually; it is important that the stone is flat to the ground with no underlying obstructions

Cutting a stone to fit the wall.

CHAPTER THREE

Planning the Garden – Surveying the Site

The project garden consisted of two levels and sloping ground. As you can see in the photographs, the predominant feature of the area is sandstone. This included the gable end of the dwelling and the high retaining wall at the back. There also existed a sandstone retaining wall, including steps. This garden is part of a Community Heritage Site, which meant that whatever was built on the ground had to be sympathetic with the area. Sympathy and blending in with surroundings is, in my opinion, a very important ethos when planning and constructing a garden. Gardens are supposed to be an area of relaxation, not just for the body and mind, but for sight also. Anything out of place instantly looks awkward, uncomfortable and therefore stresses the senses. Gardens should be stress relievers.

There is also another important point and that is to use whatever stone materials are available on site (if any), as this material usually belongs to the predominant bedrock of the area. This has the advantage of minimizing costs and also gives a base to work from. It is not always the case that you will have ready available stone, but most gardens, especially attached to older dwellings, do host some handy materials, whether from an old rockery or just old stone lying in the ground, doing nothing. Even old bricks can be used to help construct a patio's sub-base or to infill certain stone features such as a raised pond.

As you can see on the first photograph, we had an abundance of random stone, but it wasn't enough to complete the whole project. The stone was in fact old walling materials and builder's rubble, but we made use if it all. Being walling stone it was ideal for the construction of our raised pond, but not really perfect for the large patio constructed on the garden's lower level. However, the stone was utilized for the seating area, constructed above the steps on the higher section. Again not ideal as pavers, mainly due to the lack of suitable size and shape, but with adjustments to the soil levels it worked quite effectively, as later chapters will show. The point I am trying to make here is that nothing has to be wasted.

The most important exercise, before construction starts, is to know where everything is going and how it balances the whole garden. A drawing of a garden plan is essential; this can be done with garden design software on a desktop computer or by hand as a simple rough sketch. There is no need to draw up elaborate plans if you are not that way inclined, but it is one of the exciting aspects of garden construction and it will allow you to form a solid work plan and schedule. Making your plan, you need to decide what style of garden best suits your area and preferences – and this is entirely up to personal taste.

Who is going to use the garden? Is the garden for elderly people, children or families

The project garden before construction.

Top view of the project garden before construction.

with children? In all cases safety and easy access remain priorities, as does ease of movement and space. Space is just as important as the physical features. There is no point building a garden if it doesn't have enough room to enjoy it. After all, a garden is a representation of the natural open spaces, not of a city centre.

How is the garden going to be used and how do you want it to look? Apart from the human aspect of leisure, do you want to base your plot on flowers, physical features or both? Another crucial aspect is soil structure. Without soil you cannot grow plants.

ABOUT DIFFERENT SOILS

Soil is the thin layer of material on the Earth's surface in which plants have their

roots and take nutrients from the ground. Soil is formed over long periods of time, and is a mixture of rocks, minerals, dead and decaying plants, and animals. Soil can be very different in one location compared with another, but it generally consists of organic and inorganic materials, including water and air. The inorganic materials are the rocks that have been broken down by the elements into smaller pieces. They may appear as pebbles or gravel, or take smaller forms such as sand or clay. The organic material is decaying living matter: usually plants or animals that have decayed until they become part of the soil.

The amount of water in the soil is closely linked to the climate and other characteristics of the region, and will affect the amount of air the soil contains. Very wet soil – such as

21

The project garden after construction. Please note that the construction of the trellis is not described in this book.

that of wetland or marsh – has very little air. The composition of the soil affects the plants and therefore the animals that can live there.

There are three basic types of soils: clay, loamy and sandy. Loamy soils present ideal growing conditions; the remaining two types present challenges for drainage. You can use a simple exercise to find out what soil type exists in your garden. Pick up a lump of moist soil, about the size of a small ball, then roll between your thumb and finger, as if you were shaping modelling clay into a small ball. Clay soil will form a solid ball that will not crumble away. With sandy soil you will not be able to form a ball, as the soil will just disintegrate. You will begin to shape a ball with loamy soil, but it will fall away once the pressure of your finger and thumb has been released.

A second test is called a jar test and is very easy to do. You'll need a clean jam jar with a tight-fitting lid, clean water and a soil sample. Take the sample of soil (break the large clods apart so it will fit through the jar opening) and fill the jar with water until it is nearly full, but leave a small air space at the top. Screw on the lid and shake it vigorously for a minute or two, until all the soil particles are broken down into the water. Allow the suspended soil to settle for about a minute, and place a mark on the side of the jar at the top of the layer that has fallen to the bottom. This layer is comprised primarily of sand and larger particles. Set the jar aside, being careful not to mix the sand layer that has already settled, and wait approximately an hour before placing a mark on the side of the jar at the top of the next layer to settle out. This is

A computer simulation of what the garden's seating area will look like when planted up.

the silt layer. Then place the jar aside for a full day, being careful not to shake or mix the layers that have settled out. After twenty-four hours, or when the water is more or less clear, place a mark on the side of the jar at the top of the final layer. This is the clay layer. The proportions of each layer tells you what kind of soil you have.

DRAINAGE

Adequate drainage is essential in any garden, more so if you plan to install a patio or some other style of hard standing. Roofs, patios, paths and driveways create a high amount of impermeable surface area. Being aware of the impervious surfaces on your plot – and the run-off they generate – will help you design ways to reduce the negative effect your house could potentially have on the local environment. Rainwater that does not soak into the ground becomes run-off. This won't harm a patio, but it may cause damage to the surrounding area due to the high

amounts of water flow concentrated in one area. Seating areas and patios should be laid with a slight cross fall (a gentle slope), falling away from dwelling walls and neighbours' plots.

CLIMATE

Sun and shade are important factors for choosing plants. This book is not intended to be plant guide, but I have listed some interesting species that you be might consider at the back of the book.

GROUND SERVICES

Before excavating into any ground it is essential to check for underground pipes and electricity cables. Contact your local utility company to check if you will be digging near cables or gas pipes. The architect's plans of your house (if they exist, but I doubt it if your property is very old) might pinpoint where these services are.

CHAPTER FOUR

Small Sandstone Seating Area and Retaining Wall

These small seating areas are ideal for small gardens or where space is severely limited, and they can be relatively cost effective to install, too. This project featured stone already existing in the garden; some material was ideal for paving, but most of it consisted of seemingly awkward shapes. As this seating will prove, it is not very difficult to transform such material into suitable paving stones. The style of hard standing used on the seating area is called crazy paving. Crazy paving refers to the 'crazed, odd-shaped' appearance of the finished surface.

A well-laid area of paving should minimize the amount of mortar joins visible on the finished surface. The mortar is the weakest point of the area, and the less of it you use the greater the patio's chance of surviving elements like frost, snow and severe rainfall. It is very easy to lay paving with excess mortar between the pieces of stone, but this is a false economy because the area will quickly disintegrate. In most cases, crazy paving is best laid on a mortared bed, but if the stone is large enough you could actually lay them on a firm, granular soil base and then brush compost or nutrient-rich soil into the joins. This will enable the planting of aromatic groundcover plants, so when they are stepped on the aroma is released.

With natural stone (especially the material chosen for this project) you will always find a variation in thickness, as no two stones are the same shape and thickness. This results in each paving slab having to be laid on varying thicknesses of mortar to create an adequately flat walking surface.

Materials
- Around 0.5 tons of stone per square metre. The style of stone can vary and is dependent, for the most part, on your geological area. The ideal paving material is sandstone (which is the project area) or large pieces of slate. If you prefer to keep outlay to a minimum, broken concrete can be used. Old, weathered concrete can look quite natural, more so when lichen or moss has begun to take root. It doesn't, of course, lend itself to the same natural look as stone.
- Grit sand (or builders sand).
- Cement.
- Plasticizer for adding to sand and cement when pointing. This solution increases the viscosity of mix, allowing for easy, smooth pointing. An alternative is a cheap washing-up detergent. If the work is to be carried out in winter, a solution containing antifreeze is highly recommended.
- Terram membrane. This is a very fine, almost cloth-like, permeable mesh material that acts as a mulch against possible weed growth.

Tools
- Spade.
- Shovel.
- Pick or mattock.
- Lump hammer or walling hammer.
- Rubber mallet or rubber maul.
- Sledgehammer (for breaking up large stone).
- Bolster chisel (used in conjunction with hammer for accurately breaking stone).
- Large trowel.
- Pointing trowel.
- Tape measure.
- Two buckets (one for transporting mortar to the work area and the other to store small stones for pinning or gap infill).
- Cement mixer (or mixing board).
- Small hand brush (for brushing mortared joints).
- Large brush (this is used for cleaning the work area when mortar has dried).
- Scissors or carpet knife for cutting and trimming membrane.
- String line and two small stakes (optional).

Safety
- Steel toe protectors. These are available in both boots and training shoes; my assistant, who is depicted in some of the photographs, wears training shoes with steel toe caps.
- Leather safety gloves (rubber gloves will quickly shred due to the abrasive nature of natural stone).
- Eye protection (when breaking stone, shards of material can fly in any direction).

METHOD

One of the most important aspects of any paved area is a strong foundation. This isn't the mortared bed to which the stones are bonded; it is the area on which one places this bedding mixture. For small areas, such as this project, the ground should be excavated to a minimum depth of 6in (15cm), but this is dependent on the structure of your soil. What you should be aiming for is a firm layer of granular subsoil. We were lucky with this project, as the infill behind the existing retaining wall and steps was builder's rubble and hard, compacted clay. We only had to excavate down 4in (10cm) until we met a suitable foundation. This is not always the case, so it is a good idea to install a sub-base of limestone hardcore with a minimum depth of 4–6in (10–15cm), compacted down with a whacker plate. The hardcore sub-base should

Excavating the seating area's foundation.

The completed foundation.

be comprised of a 14–16in (350–400mm) layer of 'Type 1' crushed stone. Type 1 material contains stone ranging from 3in (75mm) down to dust or 'fines'. It is the fines that help to harden the sub-base. Type 1 sub-base is commonly called 'crush and run'.

Before this sub-base is installed, the mulch membrane should be laid into the foundation area, making sure it completely covers the sides of the earth walls. In almost all cases, a single run length of membrane will not be sufficient, and a second and perhaps even a third length will need to be put down. If this is the case, ensure that they bridge each other by at least 3in (75mm). On breezy or windy days, anchor the material with a quantity of stone. Note that the membrane for this project was laid on the existing, firm builder's rubble.

Depending on the angle of your slope, you might find that the foundation's excavation has created a higher, earth wall on the uphill side. This is fairly common and you should consider building up this section with a wet stone retaining wall. For higher sections you can construct the wall using the dry stone method, but this should only be carried out if you have at least four or five courses of stone to work with, otherwise the walled section will be too weak to sustain any pressure from human use. Our project seating area consist-

Laying out the edge stone that will act like shuttering and also be the foundation for the retaining wall.

ed of only three courses at its highest point, so the stone was mortared and pointed.

Laying the First Paver

Before laying the stone, the cross fall of the patio must be worked out. Rainwater will have to fall away from buildings, dwellings and neighbours' gardens. In our case the cross fall was guided toward the stone steps and the top step became part of the surface of the patio. We worked out our cross fall by placing one end of the large spirit level on the top step and building up its opposite end with stone, until the level's bubble was just past the guide line. For small paved areas a fall of 1:40 is sufficient; this means that for every 40 inches the patio descends 1 inch. When you have worked out the cross fall, a mortar mix can be made up. The weather conditions will dictate how much mortar you can mix: if it is too hot then the mixture will dry quickly and become useless. This isn't so much of problem when using a powered cement mixer, as the bucket will afford some shade and small quantities of water can be added to keep the solution moist, but if too much water is poured in the mixture may become over-moist, runny and useless to work with.

When the first mix is complete, pour a full bucket of mortar onto the middle part of the highest section (in this project's case this area was at the back of the earth bank), making sure you do not move the spirit level that is acting as the cross fall guide out of alignment. Once you have dumped the mortar in, smooth it out with a spade until you have a 2–3in (5–7.5cm) layer on the ground. This will be dependent on the size of material used, so the mixture may have to be adjusted to suit. When the stone has been bedded down its entire length should just glance the bottom of the spirit level.

Take the first paving stone, making sure its smoothest side faces upward. Bed the stone down gently with the rubber mallet or the butt of the lump hammer. In an ideal situation you should not have to pin the stone, as the mortar base should be sufficient. Given the random shape of the material, the wet mix will mould itself to the underside of the object being laid. If you have to lift the paving for any reason, you are better off re-seating it in fresh sand and cement. Once you have laid the first stone, lift the end of the spirit level and place it on this new paving, ensuring that the level still remains in place at the opposite of the work site; in the case of this project, the opposite end was the top of the existing stone step. Larger areas and working to longer cross falls will be discussed in the next chapter.

The 1:40 cross-fall for water run-off.

Important: do not, under any circumstances, tread on the crazy paving when it has just been laid and the mortar underneath is still wet.

Laying the Next Pavers

The next stones should be laid on either side of the first one and bedded into a similar depth of mortar. The important part of the task here is to ensure the joins between the stones are not too wide or too narrow. I prefer a join between 1½–2in (3.8–5cm), which will make sure there will be enough room for the mortar to do its job at the pointing phase. Too much space between the join will create a weak point where the pointing could eventually degrade and crumble.

To place a second stone, first look for the quality of surface. Bearing in mind that this project uses existing stone that was not specifically chosen, you will be choosing the best of a bad bunch, as it were. The quality to look for is a wide, flattish surface; do not worry about the shape of the underside that will be sunken into the mortar. Having found the stone, take it in two hands and place it gently at the side of the first, leaving room for the recommended pointing gap. At this time the paving should be slightly higher than the one already bedded in.

Edge stone already mortared in.

Shovelling in mortar for more edge stones.

Some edge stones may require pinning. To secure them even further, a skim of mortar can be used behind.

Level up the back of the edge stones with hearting or rubble.

Hearting at the back of the edge stones.

The completed circle of edge stones. Note how they act as shuttering. These will also form the foundation stones for the seating area's small retaining wall.

Shovelling in mortar for the first paving stones. Note the membrane that will act as a weed-excluding mulch.

Using the butt of the lump hammer to bed in the first crazy paving.

Laying the second paving stone.

On small paved areas you can use a spirit level to keep a constant check on the cross-fall.

Skimming the mortar up the side of the paving stone.

Bedding paving down using a rubber maul or mallet.

Inserting another paving stone.

Using the spirit level to check the levels on each stone.

When the mortar under the pavers is dry you can, on occasions, tread on the centre of the stones if you need to sweep away waste material.

The pavers have now been laid.

For the sake of explaining the project, we will assume that this stone was laid to the right of the original. Still holding the stone in two hands, work it gently from left to right, pushing down slightly as you go. Whilst you are doing this, continually move the stone toward the one already placed, leaving a pointing gap as described earlier. After this, take the rubber mallet or the butt of the lump hammer and carefully thump it down into the mix. Do not exert too much pressure with the hammer, otherwise you could break the material. You may find that just pushing it into the mortar is all that you need to do. Lastly, use the spirit level to inspect the cross fall and to check the levels of both stones by laying it across the two. Bed in the next stone to the left of the first paver, using the same method as just described. With a gloved hand, or a small pointing trowel, clear the joins of any mortar that is proud of the surface, making sure not to disturb the stones.

There are now three crazy paving stones laid. Complete this row following the method already described, ensuring each stone is following the cross fall. Before installing the second row, brush any mortar that has appeared on the surface into the pointing channels.

Another method for checking the level of the patio from left to right (not the cross fall) is to use a string line attached to two anchors or stakes either side of the foundation. If you are going to do this, first make sure the spirit level is set up for the cross fall, then estimate where the centre line of your next row will be and pull the string line tight so it just glances the bottom of the level. Now you only have to concentrate on the cross fall when laying the rest of the pavers. To lay the rest of the stones, follow the method I have just described.

Due to the varied size and shape of stone you will find that the material will not create a straight edge – this is obvious and it is what creates the look of crazy paving. The stones of following rows should be slotted in to fit the gaps that naturally occur. You will also note

that on some corners the pointing areas will be larger than recommended. Now is the time to choose the correct stone to fill these gaps. These smaller infill stones should be of ample depth so that at least 1in (2.5cm) can be bedded into mortar. You do not have to bed them in at this time, as this can be carried out during the pointing phase, but it is important to search for suitable material as and when the need arises, just in case it is used elsewhere. All you have to do is leave the stone resting in the gap.

When working close to the edges of the foundation trench you will probably have to trim or cut stone to fit. This isn't a difficult task and only requires a rough estimate of the size required. On most occasions you can achieve this simply by measuring the gap and marking the stone, then gently hitting it to shape with the lump hammer, trimming away the edges. If the only stone available is too large for this exercise then the use of a bolster chisel will be required to split the material.

Pointing

Ideally, when working with paving that has been laid on a mortar bed, the pointing phase should commence within three to four hours, because the mortar will still be damp within the joins and will enable a firm bond with the bedding mixture. This is fairly easy to achieve on small areas such as the project described here, but with larger patios such as that described in the next chapter the pointing will continue through to the next day and by this time the bedding mix will have started to set hard.

During hot weather it essential that the paving stones remain as damp as possible. Most natural stone material will quickly draw the moisture out of the small amount of mortar used for pointing each join before it has had time to set. This is called 'capillary action' and it will soon render your pointing dry and useless. You can counteract this by dampening the paved area with a hosepipe or a bucket of water.

Before pointing, allow the surface to dry for around an hour; exactly how long will depend on the temperature and humidity you are working in. Whilst constructing the project garden the ambient air temperature was around 90°F (32°C), but the temperature on the surface of the working area actually climbed to 120°F (49°C) due the microclimate caused by the quantity of stone in the large retaining wall and the stone walls of the dwelling, not mention the new patio. We had to continually damp down the patio, in some cases at hourly intervals.

Pointing is time-consuming work and in hot conditions it is advisable only to mix small amounts at any one time to cut down the risk of the mortar setting before you have had a chance to fill the joins. The mix should be just moist enough to enable you to roll it between your hands, forming a ball or sausage shape. If you notice water oozing between your fingers the mix is too wet. I highly recommend the use of a plasticizer added to the cement, as this creates an easy-to-work-with viscosity.

Another problem during pointing is that you will have no choice but to step on the new paving. This is worsened by the fact that the

Ready for the pointing phase of the job.

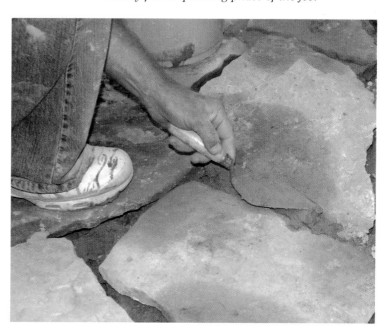

Starting the pointing.

Around half of the pointing is now complete.

Some more pointing.

Filling the pointing channel with mortar and forcing it deeply into the channel with the edge of the trowel.

After around twenty minutes of pointing, use a small brush to smooth the pointing down. Always brush in the same direction. Brushing mortar when it is too wet will result in clods being removed by accident.

stone underneath is not even, though bedded into a copious quantity of mortar. If you are pointing on the same day as laying stone it is best to begin from the front and work your way to the back: this way you will not be treading over the paving all the time. The use of a small piece of 2 × 4ft (60 × 120cm) ply board will help to disperse your weight evenly across the surface, minimizing the risk of loosening the stone. Make sure, though, that the board is free of nails, screws or dried mortar debris that could damage your pointing or the new paving stones. Surfaces that have been left overnight should be hard enough to allow careful walking on the centre of the stones, but even doing this could upset one or two pavers (if they haven't been bedded in correctly), so the use of the board is recommended here also.

A further task to do is to inspect and clear the joins of loose mortar or any debris that may have fallen in. On hot days, ensure the bedding mix within the join is kept damp, as this will decrease the risk of moisture loss from the pointing mix also.

After mixing the mortar, load some into a bucket then carry it to the pointing area. Using the trowel, scoop some mix out of the bucket, clearing away any loose mortar overhang. Next, force the mortar into the join,

ensuring that it fills any crevice caused by previously clearing the joint debris. Using the edge of the trowel, thump or tamp the pointing mix down. This is a similar technique to that used by a chef when chopping carrots, and ensures the mix is spread evenly and is tightly packed within the join. Repeat this until the entire join is full. Again, with the trowel, smooth the surface of the pointing level with the top of the paved area.

During the first phase, stone was chosen to fill larger gaps created by the random nature of the material creating wider corners than needed. When you reach these areas, lift the stone out and fill the gap with mortar. Force the stone into the gap, gently thumping it down with a rubber mallet or the butt of a lump hammer. You will find that mortar spills over the surface of the surrounding stones due to displacement by the infill stone. Quickly scrape this away to avoid staining the surface, then smooth down with the trowel.

Every twenty to thirty minutes (again, this is dependent on weather conditions) take the small hand brush then comb the new cemented joins smooth. You will find, given that your mortar was mixed correctly, that the mixture is easy to work and you should be able to create a tidy, flush surface. You should always brush in the same direction.

The completed seating area with the small retaining wall still to be built.

Repeat the procedure just described until all the joins have been filled. Cover the work area for at least twenty-four hours with a tarpaulin or similar sheet – this will protect the joins from possible overnight rain or frost. Then use a soft broom to clear the seating area of debris, brushing it in the direction of the cross fall. Take a hose pipe (with a gentle flow) or buckets of water, stand at the top of the cross fall and wash the whole area down, slowly walking to the end of the patio. You can also use the brush at the same time, but

it really is a good idea that the water flow removes most of the loose mortar and debris: this way you can avoid staining the paved area. Take note of the direction the water is travelling and of any puddles that might have formed. As mentioned earlier, the random stone used for this project was not specially chosen; it was the existing material in the garden. With material such as this you will find that some puddles will appear, but if the cross fall is correct these should be an exception rather than the rule.

CHAPTER FIVE

Large Crazy Paved Patio

Large paved areas pose more problems than the small seating area described in the previous chapter, especially when built at the side of a dwelling or bordering a neighbour's boundary. In the case of this book's example both problems occurred at once: not only did we have to build to the normal cross fall, we also had to ensure that rainwater ran away from both dwelling and garden boundaries at the same time. It was constructed with a slight cross fall of 1:40 on both sides, whereby the two falls met in the middle. The main

cross fall was 1:80 and this guided the water towards our drainage area.

Unlike the seating area, where the large spirit level was sufficient to check the cross fall, the added problems of the extra falls plus the shear surface area on this larger patio meant that a different method was required. The first stage of laying a patio of this size is to mark out the site with pegs. The pegs at the top of the proposed paved area should be set at the height of the main cross fall, whilst the pegs on either side (left

New pavers surrounding the stone seat (explained in Chapter 8). Some of the bedding mortar in this photo needs raking out of the joins.

One-quarter of the large patio has been laid.

The view from the raised pond, looking towards the existing retaining wall. Note the standing stone in the background. The raised pond is discussed in Chapter 7 and standing stones are described in Chapter 8.

Half of the pavers have now been laid for the large patio.

Two-thirds of the patio has now been laid. Note the creation of steps in the foreground. At this point the ground, although filled with builder's rubble, fell away sharply. To overcome this we created two steps to drop the level of the patio to suit the ground.

The patio viewed from the existing retaining wall. The spirit level is used to check the levels and crossfall.

All pavers for the large patio have now been bedded in and are ready for pointing. Note how the steps were created to form an aesthetic, sweeping curve. The raised pond is described in Chapter 7.

41

The completed patio. The trellis was added by me to form a windbreak and its construction is not described in this book.

A view of the completed patio, from the seating area.

to right) must reflect the height of the falls taking water away from both the dwelling and garden boundaries. The central pegs should represent the main cross fall from top to bottom. In effect, although it is not easily discernible by the eye, the entire structure forms a subtle concave shape from left to right. As a guide, use one peg every 6ft (1.8m), or else spaced so that you can easily rest timber batons.

Once the pegs have been hammered into place, the timber batons can be used as templates for each cross fall. Alternatively, you can use the large spirit level. For ease of working and room it is best only to use batons in the area you are working. Some people use string lines, but I find these get in the way, and eventually snap anyway.

The base should be prepared as described in Chapter 4. Again, we were lucky with this plot because it had already been in-filled with builder's rubble and a very hard crust of clay had already formed on the top.

When the base is ready it is time to lay the paving using the method described in Chapter 4. This time, work with the timber batons laid on the top of the pegs and ensure that the surface of the stones just glances these. When you have completed one row, move the timber over to the next working area, removing the stakes as and when required.

Due to the size of the project area, pointing was carried out over two days. A method I find beneficial, when laying large areas of crazy paving (especially when three cross falls are required), is to complete one side of the feature before starting on the next. You will see this pattern emerging in the project photographs. If you decide to work like this it is essential that the central area is not fashioned with a single straight edge, otherwise it would look odd. Leave large enough gaps between the pavings so the second half can be tied in, thus keeping the 'crazy' appearance.

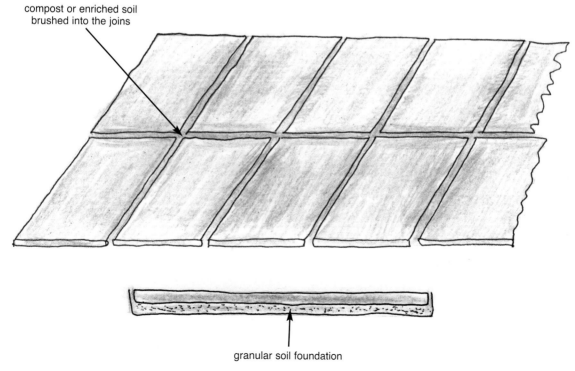

compost or enriched soil
brushed into the joins

granular soil foundation

Flag stone patio.

CHAPTER SIX

Garden Footpaths

Perhaps the most common feature in any garden with a lawn is a footpath. Paths not only offer an aesthetic aspect to a plot, they also serve an essential purpose for people who are not stable on their feet, or who are wheelchair-bound. If the lawn is part of an access point to a back gate, then you will find that people tend to walk the same route to the gate, regardless of the lawn's size. This poses a problem with erosion: the walkway soon becomes a worn, muddy track that looks unsightly and destroys a lawn. There are many options to choose from when installing a hardwearing path and it is really up to personal choice and what you feel would match your existing garden features. All paths require some form of rubble or hardcore sub-base, unless you choose to lay stone flags to create a stepping stone affair (*refer* to Chapter 9's description of flag steps, as the foundation technique is used here).

Materials
Regardless of the future load a path is going sustain, they all require a sub-base. The strongest paths are, in fact, laid with three layers: a sub-base, a base and a top surface. If a person in your family uses an invalid carriage or is wheelchair-bound, then the installation of a long-term, hardy sub-base is vital to counter any surface sinking that may occur over time.

The kind of aggregate used will depend on the nature of the surrounding soil. Limestone or chalk should not be considered in acid regions, as it will raise the local pH level, disturbing natural flora. Here you should import locally derived hardcore with a sandstone or clay-based content. As our project path is intended for infrequent, agricultural vehicular usage, the hardcore sub-base will be comprised of a 6–8in (150–200mm) layer of 'Type 1' crushed stone. This will then be compacted down using a vibrating plate. Type 1 material contains stone ranging from 3in (75mm) down to dust or 'fines'. It is the fines that help to harden the sub-base. For invalid carriages and wheelchairs the route's surface must be smooth, so the path should be surfaced with materials other than gravels. An ideal alternative is the crazy paving described in Chapter 4.

For routes constructed over soft/wet ground it is recommended that you lay a path base with a 'geotextile' membrane before hardcore is brought in. Aggregate paths will decay quickly on spongy, wet soil. A geotextile membrane counters this by creating a floating sub-surface. There are numerous geotextile products available and a list of relevant websites can be found in the Useful Contacts section.

Geotextile comes in two main types. The first type, such as 'Lotrak' and 'Terram', is a very fine-meshed, almost cloth-like permeable material similar to the membranes used for garden weed mulching. If laid correctly it allows moisture to rise upwards, preventing movement of path materials. There have been successful trials on shallow peat and mineral soils, but laid over deep, waterlogged peat it could flex, causing the path to eventually sink into the softer areas. The second type of geotextile is a stronger, rigid material such as 'Geogrids' and 'Wyretex', laid in conjunction with the fine-meshed membrane. The larger mesh styles trap the base aggregates in the wider mesh resulting in an inflexible path foundation, ideal for softer substrates. Trials over deep peat have been successful, but fine particles are able to leach through the larger grid sizes. All of these geotextile materials are more than adequate for paths that require a durable structure for continual pedestrian or wheelchair use.

Tools

- Wheelbarrow or mechanized barrow.
- Vibrating plate for compacting aggregates. Ear protection and gloves are to be worn when operating these machines.
- Large rake for levelling surfaces before compaction.
- String lines and stakes for marking path edges.
- Shovel.
- Sledgehammer.
- Tape measure.
- Long scissors or sharp knife for trimming the fabric membrane.
- Strong cutters or snips (we used tin snips) for cutting the geogrid.

For extra features such as revetments or retaining walls, use the following:

- Walling hammer.
- Claw hammer.
- Spirit level and line level.
- Crowbar.
- Fencing maul.
- Hand drill or rechargeable drill for pilot holes.

METHOD

No path construction begins without first marking the area to be excavated. This project can be anywhere from 2.5–3ft (0.75–1m) wide. The base's depth will be a minimum of 6in (15cm). Begin by staking a line either side of the proposed route. Only mark an area that can be completed in a day's work: open trenches left overnight or longer will soon become boggy in wet weather. Having marked the line with stakes, attach two parallel strings, one for each edge, and then tension them by tying them onto the end stakes. Work can begin by digging inside the string lines, until the day's foundation has been excavated.

The next phase is to lay the fabric membrane. This will come wrapped on a roll and all you need do is lift it to the start of the trench, ensuring an equal overlap on both sides. Roll the material down the line, leaving around 6in (15cm) overlapping the front of the foundation. In windy conditions you will need to use stones or some other heavy objects to weight it down; do this every 4ft (1.2m) or so. If the weather is calm the membrane can be taken to the full extent of the dig. Do not cut the membrane; leave it on the roll for the next day's dig.

If necessary, the trench is now ready for the geogrid. Geogrid sits on the bottom without any overlap. It can be quite tricky to lay due to its tendency to roll back when spread out. Again, it will require some form of weight support. Roll the grid out in stretches of around 6ft (1.8m), then import an 8in (200mm) depth of Type 1 sub-base. Extent the roll for a further 6ft and pile in more sub-base, bringing it up to the same level. As each load is dumped, it should be raked level. Try not to cover the whole section, but leave a small section of geotextile open to the air, ready for the next day's work. Doing this is essential when the geogrid has been rolled to its full extent. If it's completely covered you will not be able to overlap and tie on new grid.

Now that the sub-base has been laid and raked level, use the vibrating plate to firm it down. Following the edge of the trench, start from one end, guiding the machine to the

excavated foundation trench -
minimum depth 6in (15cm)

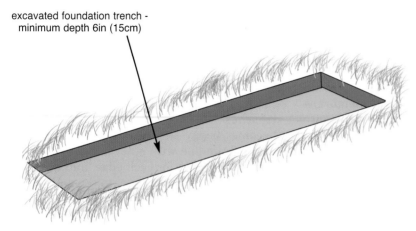

*Stages of gravel footpath
construction (1).*

hardcore sub-base to a
height of 4in (10cm)

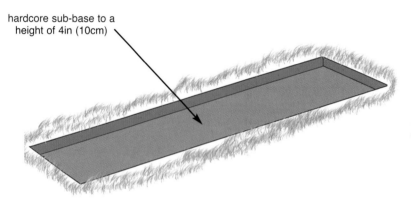

*Stages of gravel footpath
construction (2).*

it is important to adequately
compact the sub-base using
a mechanical compactor

gravel surface laid on the
sub-base to just above
the level of the surrounds

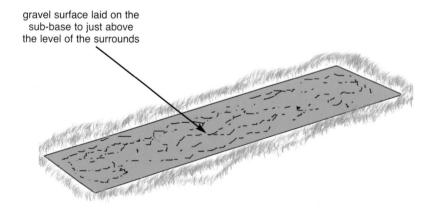

*Stages of gravel footpath
construction (3).*

Sections of a garden path.

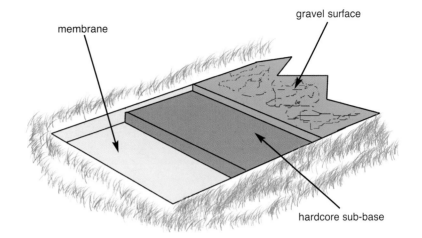

membrane

gravel surface

hardcore sub-base

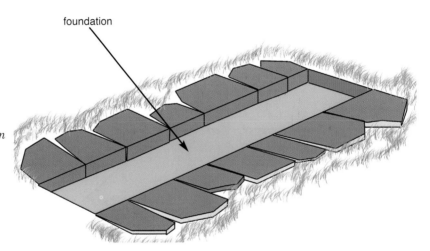

foundation

*Gravel footpath construction
using edging stones (1).*

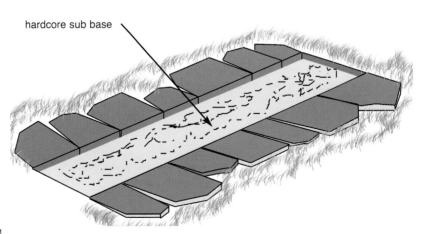

hardcore sub base

*Gravel footpath construction
using edging stones (2).*

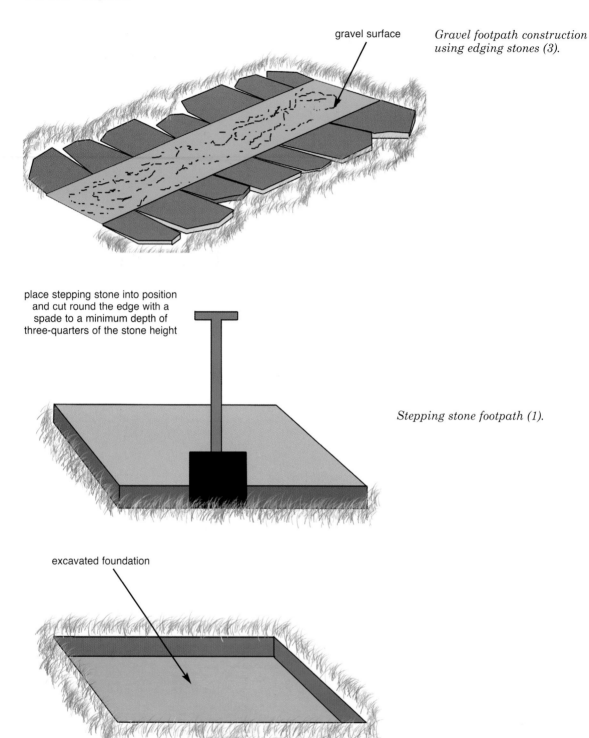

gravel surface

Gravel footpath construction using edging stones (3).

place stepping stone into position and cut round the edge with a spade to a minimum depth of three-quarters of the stone height

Stepping stone footpath (1).

excavated foundation

Stepping stone footpath (2).

Stepping stone footpath (3).

place stepping stone into the
excavated foundation and bed
down using a rubber maul

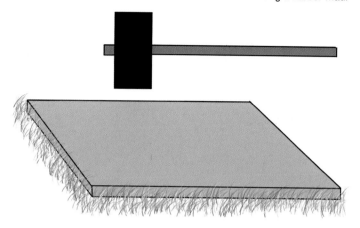

repeat as necessary for the
length of the footpath

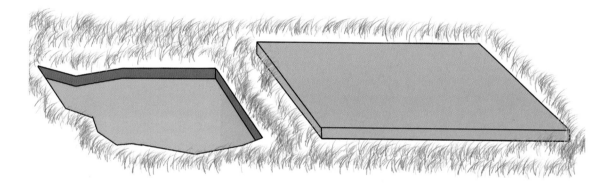

Stepping stone footpath (4).

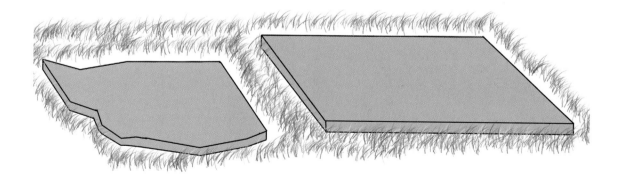

Stepping stone footpath (5) – completed.

opposite end. Turn around then make your way back to the beginning, working a fresh line next to the one just compacted. Continue in this fashion, gradually moving toward the opposing edge, until the entire section has been tamped. That was one 'pass'; at least five passes are necessary to ensure sufficient compaction.

That has just described a hardwearing path sub-base that is now ready to accept your chosen surface materials. As I suggested earlier, this is really up to personal choice, but if a smooth walkway is not an issue then there are many ornamental gravels on the market that can be used as walking surface. Many quarries and stone suppliers (there is a list of contacts at the back of this book) will offer viable alternatives such as slate chippings or sandstone rubbles, any one of which will suit a natural stone theme. Alternatively, if you have constructed a crazy-paved seating area or patio, perhaps your path surface can utilize this style. If so, follow the instructions given

in Chapter 4 as the laying technique is exactly the same.

There is a very interesting, ancient method of creating a hardy surface and that is called stone pitching. This surface is so durable that countryside professionals are now installing it on popular, well-walked footpaths. My book, *Building Countryside Paths and Tracks*, also published by Crowood, explains this in more detail.

PATH SURFACING

There are many styles of footpath surface to choose from, the most popular being ornamental gravels. These, needless to say, are inadequate for persons who find walking difficult and for people in wheelchairs or invalid carriages. Gravels, none the less, can play an important role in adding a diversity of stone colour in a garden constructed from a single stone source, such as slate or sandstone. The one drawback with gravel is the high mainte-

Paths without a solid sub-base will soon deteriorate.

Erosion caused by continual walking on the same area.

nance and cost associated with aggregate loss due to people or pets accidentally kicking the material away from the walking area. Installing a permanent edging will eliminate some of the problem, but won't solve it completely. So, if you have children or animals that like to run around the garden (as they regularly do) a hardier alternative may be required.

Stone pitching is a very interesting, ancient method of creating a hardy walking surface. It is so durable that countryside professionals have now started to resurface well-worn and popular walking routes using this method.

Alternatively, a long-lasting path surface can be created utilizing the crazy-paving technique described in Chapter 4.

Gravel Surfacing

Ornamental gravel comes in many colours and sizes, and which one is chosen really is up to personal taste. These aggregates tend to be on the expensive side, and cheaper alternatives can be purchased from quarries as slate, limestone or sandstone fines. The least expensive material is the grey gravel used for creating concrete, which can be found in any builder's merchant. Regardless of style, all gravel is laid in exactly the same way, with at least 3–4in (7.5–10cm) covering the sub-base.

Materials
A half ton of gravel should be suitable to cover most domestic garden paths.

Tools
• Wheelbarrow.
• Rake.
• Shovel.

Method
Compared with the alternative path coverings, gravel is the quickest and easiest to lay, and the surfacing job can be finished in a

matter of hours. To begin, shovel a barrow-full of aggregate and take it to the furthest end of the new path, dumping it in the middle of the sub-surface. Using the rake, gently push the gravel to all the edges, creating an even layer. Next, wheel in a second barrow load and pour it onto the sub-surface, leaving a 2ft (60cm) gap between the first layer, and rake level as just described. Continue in this fashion until the path has been surfaced.

Stone Pitched Surface

A stone pitched path does not require a sub-base if it can be installed on a firm, granular soil foundation. If your garden's subsoil is too soft then a sub-base, similar to the one described earlier, must be installed to counter any future sinking of the path. The stone pitching technique is very similar to dry stone walling (explained later) and almost the same as laying crazy paving (explained in Chapter 4). It involves the positioning of large, undressed stone on the path line to create a walkway. The stones are dug into the subsoil with a flat face uppermost, wedged together to give mutual strength, and any gaps are back-filled and then covered with soil.

Materials

- 1 ton of large random stone for every 12ft (3.6m) on a path 3ft (1m) in width.
- Membrane for weed control.
- Builder's sand. (You will need this if you are pitching over a hardcore sub-base, as the stone will require bedding in.)

Tools

- Walling hammer or lump hammer.
- Bolster chisel.
- Spade.
- Bucket.
- Rubber maul.
- Spirit level.
- String line.

This path and step affair was laid using the 'stone pitching' technique. Stone pitching is a method where pavers are set into a granular soil foundation and packed with hearting stone or rubble infill. This is a very old-fashioned style that has now become very popular with countryside professionals. Many countryside paths and hard-standing areas are constructed using the stone pitching method.

*Close-up of stone pitched path. This is laid in very similar fashion to the crazy
paving described earlier. Stone is so tightly packed within the foundation that
very little (if any) movement occurs. What is more, stone pitched areas can survive
the rigours of nature, unlike mortared affairs that probably have a lifespan of
around twenty years.*

- Large brush.
- Four 2ft × 2in × 2in stakes.
- Tape measure.
- Rake.

Method

(The following description assumes you are stone pitching on granular soil)

Firstly, excavate a foundation as described earlier in this chapter. The trench should be at least 5in (12.5cm) in depth, but no deeper than 6in (15cm). After completing the excavation work, ensure the base of the trench is as level and as firm as possible. Ramming in small stone can compact any soft areas. It is important to store the dug-out topsoil, as a quantity of this will be needed to brush into the path surface's gaps when the job is complete.

Place a large stone into a corner of the foundation, ensuring it is touching the edges of the trench and its widest surface area is facing downward, and then bed it down with the rubber maul. You will need to check this stone with the spirit level as you settle it in. Take a second large stone and lay it in the next corner, at the same end of the sub-base. Again, bed it in with the maul and use the spirit level. After this, place a third large stone against the inside, front edge of the trench, but this time make sure it is abutting tightly to either of the first two. Using the walling hammer or lump hammer, ram in and force smaller material in the gaps. It is important that this is a tight fit. The latter action will push the larger stones against the foundation's earth walls, countering any possible, future movement. Repeat this procedure at the opposite end of the foundation trench.

With the two ends of the path now firmly bedded in, the remaining stone surface can be laid. Working from one end, bed in large stone (as described earlier) against both edges of the trench, working alternately from one side and then the other, and ensuring the material's length is running toward the centre of the path. It is vital that the edges of the path host the largest material, so you must ensure that the larger surfacing stone is laid in accordance with this. The central gaps between the edge stones should be laid with stone large enough to totally fill these areas and, if possible, the material should abut the existing surface material. Smaller gaps must be packed with hammered-in stone.

To finish the job, load topsoil into the bucket, pour it into all of the path surface's joins and use the large brush to make sure it is accurately swept in. Vegetation will grow back naturally, but you may want to sow aromatic, ornamental, ground-cover plant seeds. There are two main benefits associated with this. Firstly, plants or grasses will help to further bind and secure the path surface; and secondly, aromatic ground cover will produce pleasant odours when walked on.

Stepping-Stone Path

A stepping-stone path, running across a lawn, is the most basic and straightforward of walking surfaces to install. It does not require the laborious excavation of a long foundation trench, as each stone sits in its own shallow, easy to dig, granular soil base. Furthermore, if one does not have the confidence or time to embark on a major construction project, which could span several days, stepping-stones offer a viable and durable alternative. One of the major drawbacks with building long paths is the open foundation that is at the mercy of inclement weather. Rain will soon create a muddy trench, especially if it has to be left overnight or longer. A stepping-stone project, on the other hand, can be carried out piecemeal because each stone is an independent, bedded-in object. As soon as one stone is laid, the foundation is covered, until the next one is dug out.

Materials
To produce a stable walking surface the stone has to be substantial, with a surface area large enough to displace the weight and pressure of constant use. The ideal material is stone of around 2 × 2ft (60 × 60cm), but this is just a rough guide and minimum dimensions of 1½ × 1½ft (45 × 45cm) would just about meet the requirements. Broken flagstones offer the safest and most stable paving qualities, as their surfaces tend to be smooth and flat, which makes them easy to lay.

Tools

- Spade.
- Rubber maul.
- Rubber mallet.
- Rake.
- Spirit level.

Method
After choosing your route, lay the first stone on the ground, in the exact position it is going to be bedded in. Work your way around the paving stone with the spade, pushing it into the ground no more then 2–3in (50–75mm). This will be dependent on the thickness of the material, so use the latter as a general guide. Remove the stone, then excavate a foundation no deeper than the depth of the stone, then loosen up the subsoil with the rake. If you are working across a lawn, place the removed turf to one side, as you will need some small slithers to help firm up later. Next, lift the paving into the prepared hole, ensuring a tight fit. Taking the maul, hammer the stone down to bed it in, checking the length and breadth with the spirit level.

To finish this section, cut thin lengths of turf with the spade, and then force them down the sides of the stepping-stone with the rubber mallet. Lastly, test the stone by walking on it. Some slight movement may be detected, but it should not pose much of a problem, for when the vegetation around the edges grows back it will help to bond the paving to the ground.

CHAPTER SEVEN

Raised Ponds

A pond is a small ecosystem in its entirety and can provide a resource for in-depth study, for children, into species identification, habitats, diversity, food chains and so on. Water also attracts useful predator species such as frogs and toads, which are beneficial to the garden. On the question of safety, a raised pond eliminates the possibility of a child accidentally falling in (they have to climb the walls first) and a grille can be fitted across

the surface to provide additional protection. The grille, however, should be large enough so it will not interfere with water plants and wildlife. One thing that fascinates me about creating water features is the fact that life appears and grows without any human input whatsoever. You build the pond, fill it with water and then let nature do the rest.

There is not a fixed requirement as regards the length and width of the pond, but

Slate pond – a raised pond constructed out of Welsh Blue Slate. This project was part of a primary school garden I designed and constructed in 1997.

for a healthy ecosystem to exist the depth is important, as plants and wildlife require a certain level of water. Water lilies and fish require a minimum depth of 1ft (30cm); 2ft (60cm) at the deepest point is best, as this prevents the water freezing completely in winter. The marginal plants require no more than 9in (23cm) and most even less. We constructed our project pond with a number of shallow areas of a slightly differing depth; the deep area had a maximum depth of 18in (45cm).

Tools

- Spade.
- Shovel.
- Pick or mattock.
- Walling hammer or lump hammer.
- Large trowel.
- Pointing trowel.
- Spirit level.
- Tape measure.
- Scissors or carpet knife.
- Sledgehammer.

Materials

- Sand and cement.
- Plasticizer.
- Butyl pond liner.
- Natural stone.

METHOD

Ideally, a raised pond should be sighted in a position where it can be easily walked around and viewed from all sides. Try to avoid building it (or any pond for that matter) underneath or close to trees, otherwise leaf fall during autumn will contaminate the pond water: autumn leaves that have fallen into pond water will become a mouldy, slimy mess, and debris in the water such as leaves and twigs will upset the condition of your pond and possibly kill off essential water-faring wildlife. If you have no choice but to construct the pond in the vicinity of trees, then you could purchase a tarpaulin or canvas cover to use during the autumn period.

Another important feature of the raised pond is the overflow: excess water will have to be released somewhere. Overflow occurs when rainwater naturally tops up the existing surface water and is then released through a planned outlet, usually near the deepest section. The water overflow is normally equal to the amount of rainwater falling into it, assuming there are no extra pressures from dripping trees or run-off from buildings. Overflows have to happen and it really isn't as bad as it sounds, especially with small raised ponds such as this. Most of the time you probably won't even notice when it is overflowing, as it will only form a trickle in all but the worst downfalls, but then the surrounding area is receiving far more from the heavens than from your raised pond anyway.

As the project pond is an essential feature of the large, crazy-paved area, the overflow was designed to run down the pond wall onto the patio, then flow with the area's cross fall. The only problem to be careful of here is algae build-up, and the cleaning of this should be planned in as part of an annual maintenance routine.

Marking the Ground and Preparing the Foundation

One of the important things to work out first is, what shape would you like your pond to be? Is going to be circular, oval or square? (Personally, I feel that square raised ponds in natural stone look too cumbersome.) Oval is a good aesthetic shape if you have enough available stone. At the request of the garden's owner, who wanted something to resemble an extremely old well, we installed a circular raised pond, 6ft (1.8m) across by 3¼ft (1m) deep. Having ascertained your shape, the next job is to mark the ground with this shape in mind. You can do this by using some rope or a length of old hosepipe. With the shape marked on the ground, use the spade and push it into the soil, marking the entire

Preparing the raised pond's foundation. The foundation should have a minimum depth of 6in (15cm).

Using a bucket to pour concrete into the raised pond's foundation.

Using the hammer to bed the foundation stones into the mortar.

Backfill the course of stones with hearting (loose rubble) and a copious skim of mortar.

Large stones can be pinned from behind if the stone needs levelling or if it wobbles.

On occasion, some stones may need to be trimmed or cut to size so they can fit on the course. Use the tape measure to gauge how much material you will need to cut away, then score a deep line with the bolster chisel. Next, working down the line, use both lump hammer and chisel to break the stone down the line.

The newly cut stone can now be moved into position.

When the foundation stones have been laid, skim their backs with mortar.

The completed raised pond foundation; note the amount of mortar skim.

perimeter, then discard the rope/hosepipe.

The foundation for the pond should be at least 6in (15cm) in depth and around 6–8in (15–20cm) wide. It is worth mentioning now that the project pond was constructed before the large patio was installed, and although the pond's foundation was 6in in depth, an extra 5in (7.5cm) was added due to the mortar and paving materials of the surrounding area.

When the foundation has been excavated, the soil can be dumped into the centre of the pond area. One end of this will need to be raised anyway for the pond's shallow section. Having finished this phase, a ratio of 1 part cement, 3 parts builder's sand and 1 part gravel (or small stone that may be lying around) can be mixed then poured into the circular trench.

Building the Pond Walls

The first course of stone is the most important for any type of random stone wall, as this is going to hold the weight of the entire structure. Where raised ponds are concerned the initial course not only has to secure the weight of the material on top, it must also be able to hold the secondary weight of the volume of water. As with any random wall these first stones have to be the largest of your supply and sit on a bed of freshly mixed mortar. It does not matter where in the foundation trench the initial stone is laid, the important thing is to remember to follow basic walling techniques (described in more detail in Chapter 10).

Carefully place the stone on the bed of mortar, then gently manoeuvre its face to line up with the outer wall of the foundation trench.

On some courses the top of the stones may be too thin to allow a stable layer on top. If this is the case, build up the back using mortar and smaller stone.

Mortar has been placed onto the course and is now ready for stone to be laid on top.

Laying the pond's second course of stones. The nature of random stone means that ideal 'brick-shapes' are very rare. Note the angular shape of this stone.

The use of pinning stone will help to level and support angular-shaped stone.

The fact the raised pond's outer wall is a weight-bearing structure means that just one pinner is not sufficient. The underneath of the stone must be completely packed with smaller material.

After packing the stone apply a thick mortar skim and smooth it down using the trowel.

The stone is now firm enough for a course to be laid on top.

The raised pond has now been built to the penultimate course of walling stone. Note how the rubble on the inside-right of the pond has helped to create the shallow area.

Using the rubber mallet or the butt of a lump hammer, gently tap the stone into the mix until it feels firm in the mortar. Depending on the weight of the stone, you may be able to bed it in by just pushing down with both on hands. The top surface should be as even as possible to enable the second course to be built on top, so if the stone appears to angle too much away from the centre of the structure you will not be able to lay a secure row on top. Either turn the stone around and try it different ways or discard it and find another, but be mindful of the fact that this rock may have to be used anyway. If the worst comes to the worst and the only way to use it is to have a surface sloping into the structure, then this is quite acceptable, as hearting and mortar can be used to bring it up to a workable, stone-laying height.

Before laying a second foundation stone, take a large trowel's worth of mortar and skim it up the side of the first one, where the join between first and second will be. Next, lay the second stone in the same manner as the first, only this time gently force it against the mortar skim to create a bond. If cement oozes from the join, rake it out with the trowel or a gloved hand and chuck the waste onto the course, ready for the third stone. Lay the remaining foundation stones using this method until this first course is complete. Lastly, shovel mortar behind each foundation stone and, using the large trowel, skim it toward the top of the course, filling all gaps. Larger gaps are better filled with a hearting and cement mixture. This will bind everything together to create a secure first layer.

The nature of random stone will, in most cases, create a course of varying levels; this is quite normal. So, to begin the second course, it is essential to build up these gaps first. This job may only involve the addition of one or two smaller face-stones, laid on mortar, to raise the course level. Once you have done this, the second course of stones can be mortared into place. This is essentially the same technique used for the foundation, but the vital part is to ensure that lower joints, created by the first course, are crossed (or bridged) by the second course. Like the foundation, this second layer must be bonded by a cement back-skim and larger gaps filled with a mortar and hearting mix.

Construct the remaining courses using the method just described. If possible, try to use smaller stone on the higher rows, as this will make levelling the structure easier. If you haven't already chosen the area for the pond's shallow end, now would be a good time to do it, because as the pond is built higher, the mortar back-skim generally becomes difficult to achieve. Knowing where the different depths are going means you can begin to use infill material to build the level up to the planned shallow end. When the pond has been constructed to three-quarters of its finished height some form of guide for the proposed water level would be useful. You can achieve this simply by knocking in two rods or canes, either side of the structure, then stretching and tying a string line between the two. This line can also be utilized as guide for the penultimate course of building stone, the layer that will be used to create the overflow and hold the edges of the pond liner. Obviously a last row of stones will be mortared on top, but this is installed after the liner has been correctly fitted.

Important note: the width of the pond wall during this next phase should, if possible, remain at a good 5in (12.5cm) buildable width. If some stones appear too narrow then they should be laid in pairs, one behind the other, to create the required minimum width.

After setting up the string line the remainder of the pond walls can now be laid. Build the pond's wall to within one course of the string line, levelling the stone as much as you can with pinning and mortar. At this point it is not critical that all the stones are flush with the wall's top edge, but during the next course the use of the spirit level is essential to help create a level perimeter for the pond liner. It is now important not to use material that will increase the height above the string line, so the correct choice of stone is vital. The

Checking the levels with a spirit level.

advantage of using mortar means that the wall can be made level by using varying thicknesses of the mix under each stone; this is an acceptable technique and the only one that will work with random-sized materials. Whilst laying this level course choose the section for your overflow (if you haven't done so already), remembering that the water must leave the pond from the deep end and not the shallow area. Do not put mortar on a stone here.

Lining the Pond

The basic shell of the pond has now been constructed and infill has been placed inside to help fashion the deep end and shallow area. The next job is to sculpture the inside with mortar. If the sand and cement supply is running low, the most important area to shape is the deep end, for the pond wall here is at its weakest and it is structurally essential for the back of this wall to be strong. Having mixed the mortar, take a bucket-full and pour it into the deep end. Using the large trowel, push the mix up the back of the stones, ensuring that all the holes are completely filled. Repeat until you have shaped a concave,

mortared well. Be careful, however, not to lose too much pond depth. If there is enough mix, try to skim the shallow area also. Leave to set for around four hours.

The next stage of the job is to line the entire pond area with builder's sand; everything that the pond liner will touch must be thickly covered. To effectively perform this next job the sand should be dampened down so it can stick to the mortar skim and can be easily shaped by hand. Start by dumping two or three bucket-loads of sand into the deep area. Then, using a hand, rake it over the surface of the mortar until it leaves at least a 2in (5cm) layer. Repeat this until the pond has a total blanket of sand. Next, pat the sand down until it forms a solid-looking shell. The next part of this task is to sculpture some flat planting areas on the slope leading toward the shallow end. Planting shelves should be at least 5in (12.5cm) below the waterline. With this in mind, shovel some damp sand into the bucket and transfer it by hand into the shallow area. Just shaping and patting is all that is required to create stable shelves, and you will find that it is very easy to achieve.

To further secure the pond's outer shell a complete skin of mortar is applied to the inside of the entire structure. Note the shallow and deep ends.

Another view of the mortar-lined pond.

The pond must now be lined with a 2in (5cm) layer of damp sand. Note the load of sand dumped into the deep area.

Using a hand, rake the sand toward the top of the pond and then pat it down to form a smooth surface.

Creating a planting shelf out of sand.

The pond has now been completely lined with damp sand, with sharp edges covered. Sharp areas may rip the pond liner, although this is fairly rare when using butyl. Do it as a precaution anyway.

A wide range of liners is available and many have a twenty-year guarantee against ultraviolet light decay. The strongest liners are made of butyl. Butyl liners, although slightly more expensive than alternative materials, offer good protection against tree root penetration (not an issue with raised ponds of course) and accidental puncturing by ornaments that may fall in. To install the liner, measure the length and width of the pond at its surface and the deepest part of the pond to the surface, then calculate the amount of liner required using this formula: (length + twice the depth) × (width + twice the depth).

The liner can now be rolled over the pond, ensuring that there is a good overlap on all sides of at most 12in (30cm); the excess will be trimmed away later. Push the liner into the deep end, ensuring that it is touching the sand underneath. Don't worry if the liner creases – this cannot be helped on small ponds where the shallow end suddenly falls away to the deep end. Add a layer of sand or subsoil (not topsoil) to protect and hide the liner and provide a growing medium for the plants.

Filling the Pond

Fill your pond with a hosepipe by letting the water trickle in gently so that it does not disturb the subsoil. As the pond is filling, check for air bubbles under the liner and push them upward and out with your hand. Ensure the edges of the liner do not fall into the water and, as a precaution, work your way around the entire perimeter of the pond to continually pull the liner tight. Where the overflow is situated, place some loose stones under the liner to raise it above the top edge of the course of stones. Continue filling until the pond is full: the water should cover the shallow area in its entirety. Working on the overflow again, remove one loose stone at a time until the pond begins to spill. You are not looking for a 'gush' here, merely a steady

The butyl liner has now been inserted into the raised pond and a hosepipe is slowly filling it with water.

Whilst the pond is filling, use your hand to force any air bubbles upwards and outwards.

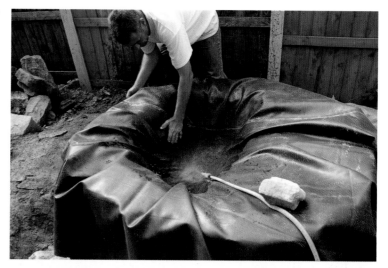

Releasing more air bubbles.

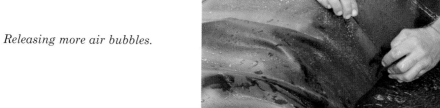

Stretching the pond liner as it is filling with water.

The pond has now been filled and will be left for twenty-four hours to give any leaks a chance to reveal themselves.

Trimming the excess butyl liner.

trickle. As soon as this has been achieved, strengthen the overflow by packing in more stone, ensuring not to build up the height.

The final job of this phase is to trim the pond liner back to the outside edge of the wall, so that it just covers the top stones. The raised pond should now be left for around twenty-four hours just in case it has a leak – highly unlikely with butyl, but this is just a precaution. It is much easier to drain the pond to get a replacement liner now without having to remove the mortared coping stones that secure the liner to the structure.

Tying the Liner to the Pond

Assuming there are no problems with leaks, the pond liner must now be secured to the structure. This is achieved by cementing a final layer of coping stones onto the pond wall. The coping is mortared to the wall, but at the same time it has to tie or jam the pond liner between the two courses. One cannot dump a mix onto the butyl material and hope for a firm bond; it just will not happen. The correct method is to fold the liner toward the pond, leaving half of the top surface of the stone available for bonding. From then on it

Securing the raised pond's top stones (or coping stones). Note how the butyl liner is folded back to reveal the stone surface. The mortar should cover the bare stone and the liner. Make sure that no cement falls into the water.

Carefully laying a top stone.

Bedding in a top stone using hand pressure.

Pin and carefully trowel a mortar skim to the back of the top stones. Again, ensure that no mixture falls into the water.

The raised pond's overflow. Note how this section has been left dry, free from mortar; this allows for subtle adjustments to the water level. As soon as you are happy with the waterline, the area surrounding the overflow can be cemented up.

is just a matter of choosing suitable stones and bedding them into cement, using the technique described for building the pond itself. Try not to drop too much mortar into the pond water otherwise you may have to drain and refill again. It is important during this phase that the overflow section remains free from cement.

The last construction phase is pointing the joins. This is basically the same method described for pointing the crazy paving in Chapter 4. You will, however, be pointing vertically as opposed to horizontally, so a slight-

ly different technique will be required. After mixing the mortar, scoop some onto the large trowel. Next, using the small trowel, cut off any overhanging mix. Take the large trowel to where you want to point and hold it against the join. With the small pointing trowel, push the mix into the join, ensuring it fills it completely, then smooth it down with the pointing trowel's flat blade. At twenty-minute intervals, use the hand brush to further smooth the new mortared joins, ensuring that you brush in one direction only. Carry on like this until the entire raised pond has been pointed.

Pointing the pond's walls. Place a load of mortar onto the large trowel, take it the area you are pointing, then use the small trowel to force the mortar into the pointing channel.

Smoothing the pointing down with the pointing trowel.

New pointing on the pond's walls.

To help hide the pond liner you can use some ornamental stone to create a beach effect in the shallow end.

The completed pond with the pointing drying.

A view of the top of the pond showing top stones and ornamental beach.

Showing the pond's beach from a different angle.

Pond plants help to bring colour and life to any water feature.

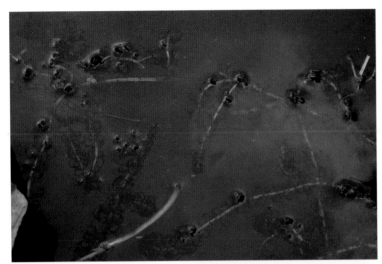

Oxygenating plants help produce oxygen for pond life and stop the water from becoming stagnant. These plants are ideal if the water feature does not contain a fountain or waterfall.

Adjusting the pond's overflow for the last time.

Cementing up and pointing the area around the raised pond's overflow.

Tap water is full of nutrients and so algae are likely to colonize the pond initially, turning the water green. At first this may appear disturbing and ugly: do not worry, it will settle down as nutrient levels fall. You should leave the pond for around one week before planting.

OTHER STYLES OF WATER FEATURE BASED ON NATURAL STONE

Pebble Pool

In recent years pebble pools have become very popular; they represent a highly cost-effective alternative to large ponds. For people who can't be bothered with the extra maintenance of a raised or sunken pond, but still want a water feature to complement their garden, pebble pools – large or small –

are a viable alternative. Complete DIY kits can be purchased from most garden centres and DIY stores. These kits contain everything you need except the stone, but this material can be found in such outlets, too.

The only possible complication with these features is the installation of the water pump. The pool will have to be sited close to an electrical source and the pump's cable must be buried underground within a conduit and connected to the mains or an adequate circuit breaker. Other than that the pool is very simple to install. Of course you do not have to buy it as a ready-made kit, you can actually create your own by using some everyday things you might have lying around the garage or home. Instead of a pump that requires a mains supply, there are many solar-powered versions available. The more expensive solar pumps actually come with

Large raised pond – a large, slate raised pond and patio I constructed in 2000.

batteries that charge via the solar cell or can be topped up from your normal, household mains when sunlight is in short supply, as it invariably is in the UK and many other countries in the northern hemisphere. The following projects are based on solar-powered, submersible pumps.

This style of water feature is a way of bringing water into your garden if a raised pond or open water feature is neither possible nor desirable, especially if you have issues of safety where young children are concerned. A pebble pool is quick and easy way to install and has a varied design opportunity to suit most garden plots.

A pebble pool can be circular, rectangular or square, but all host a central reservoir (or sump) area and a wide flange to catch the falling water and direct it back into the sump. The reservoir holds water that is circulated by the small, submersible pump. These fea-tures are available in a range of sizes, and whilst the most common types are a light-weight moulded plastic, heavier-duty glass-fibre versions are available that can include heavy features like small standing stones that have been pre-bored (or drilled) to form a fountain. A large version of this is described later.

Creating a Feature from a Pebble Pool

The flange and reservoir lid are usually cov-ered with cobbles of various sizes so as to completely hide the black plastic underneath. A fountain spray or geyser effect can be gen-erated directly from the submersible pump in the reservoir. Alternatively, a hose can be fed from the pump and attached to any number of items such as drilled boulders or pots, ornamental fountains, slate or granite columns (explained later).

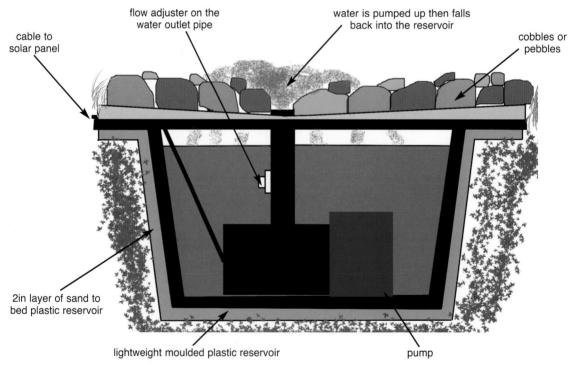

A pebble pool.

Materials

- Pebble pool kit.
- Sand.
- Corbels/pebbles.
- Solar-powered submersible pump.

Tools

- Spade.
- Tape measure.
- Spirit level.
- Rubber mallet.

Method

After choosing a suitable area for the pool, excavate the hole for the moulded plastic reservoir. This should at least 2in (5cm) wider and deeper than the overall size of the sump. Take note of the sump's flange: this should rest on the surrounding ground, so do not excavate wider than this. After completing the hole, pack it tightly on all sides with damp sand, using the method described for the raised pond earlier. Take some extra sand and give the area surrounding the topside of the hole a good 2in (5cm) layer. Next, drop the reservoir into the hole, ensuring that it is a tight but easy fit and that the flange is resting on the surrounding sand. Take the spirit level and lay it across the pool; if it is not level, gently tap it into the sand using a rubber mallet.

With the pool now in position, insert the solar pump and find a nearby sunny position for the solar cell. Once this is done, fill the reservoir with clean tap water and switch the pump on to test it. You may need to adjust the 'head' pressure; there is usually a small, plastic tap situated on the pump's outlet pipe for this purpose. (The term 'head' means the maximum distance a pump will push water, which varies with the power of the machine.) To minimize splashing and water loss I would suggest a head of no more than 2in (5cm). Assuming the pump is in good working order, place the concave lid onto the top of the reservoir, ensuring the pump's outlet pipe is pro-

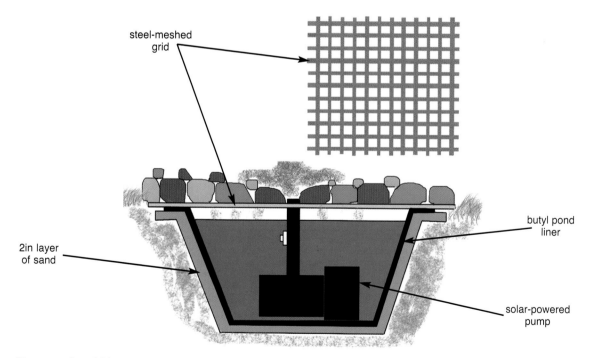

steel-meshed grid

2in layer of sand

butyl pond liner

solar-powered pump

Home-made pebble pool.

truding from the lid's central hole. Lastly, carefully site your chosen pebbles, taking care not to disturb the pump's pipe. As a finishing touch, cover the solar cell cable with gravel or more pebbles.

Home-Made Pebble Pool

The cheaper alternative to purchasing plastic moulded materials is to make your own reservoir with some butyl pond liner and placing a steel grid on top to hold the pebbles. It is simple, effective and very easy to build.

Materials

- Enough butyl pond liner to line an excavation 12in (30cm) deep and 12in (30cm) wide.
- Sand.
- Solar-powered submersible pump.
- 13 × 13in (33 × 33cm) steel grid, with 1in (2.5cm) squares. You should be able to find something like this at a scrapyard – one alternative is find an old fireguard (not a spark guard) and cut the mesh down to size.

Tools

- Spade.
- Tape measure.
- Spirit level.

Method

After choosing you ideal site, begin by excavating the reservoir. In this case, 12in (30cm) deep by a maximum of 12in wide. Line the reservoir with damp sand, using the same technique as described for the raised pond. Next, lay the butyl liner into the hole, ensuring a decent overlap over the surface of the soil. Fill with water and insert the pump. Find a sunny location for the pump's solar cell and test the flow. Adjust the flow until you achieve a 2in (5cm) head of water. Dig the overhanging liner into the surrounding soil, ensuring not to damage the pool walls, then lay the steel grid over the top, making sure the pump's outlet pipe is protruding

upward. Lastly, place pebbles onto the grid, eventually hiding the steel squares.

Maintaining a Pebble Pool

As there is not an open body of water or fish to produce waste, maintaining a pebble pool should be easy with minimal attention. A mild, environmentally safe algicide will help to prevent algae build-up over the cobbles but it may still, on occasion, be necessary to remove them for a scrub in a bucket of water. One of the best ways to ensure minimum maintenance is to choose a pump for the feature that is capable of handling small solids and does not have a sponge foam intake. This is especially important with constructions that have a heavy fountain feature. Check the water level regularly, as splashing and evaporation, especially in hot weather, can quickly deplete the contents of the relatively small reservoirs. If the water level drops so as to expose the pump then there is a risk of the pump seizing up.

Medium-Sized Standing Stone Waterfall

This next idea can look very effective as part of a natural stone garden that incorporates a stone circle similar to this book's main project, and will make a safer, child-friendly alternative to a raised pond. Specially drilled (or pre-bored) stone can be purchased from any garden centre and is available in a range of sizes. The following project describes a similar feature I installed in a local Youth Partnership garden some years ago. It is safe, almost vandal-proof and very strong, to the point that if stood on by accident it will not cause any damage.

Materials

- 1 × 3ft (1m) pre-bored standing stone. (These are very heavy and it took three of us to lift it onto the finished reservoir.)
- 2 tons of natural, random walling stone.
- Sand and cement.
- Butyl pond liner.

*Standing stone waterfall –
reservoir.*

the walls of the reservoir are constructed in the same style as the raised pond, but the height of the feature should be around 1½–2ft (45–60cm)

the internal section is lined with sand then the liner is laid in the same fashion as the raised pond's liner

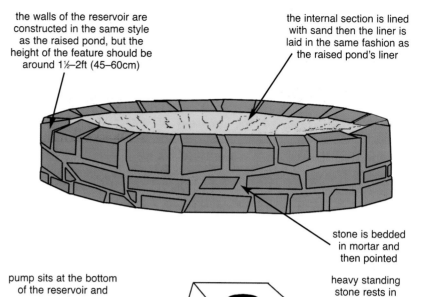

stone is bedded in mortar and then pointed

pump sits at the bottom of the reservoir and water is pushed to the top of the stone and then trickles back into the sump

heavy standing stone rests in welded steel frame

*Standing stone waterfall –
welded frame.*

frame sits on the reservoir walls. the last course of stone hides the steel

standing stone drilled for pond-pump hose

water trickles out of the top of the stone and falls back into the reservoir

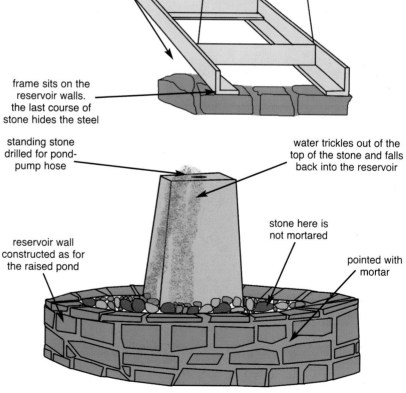

reservoir wall constructed as for the raised pond

stone here is not mortared

pointed with mortar

*Standing stone waterfall –
complete.*

- 1 solar-powered, submersible pump with a head of at least 4ft (1.2m).
- 5in (12.5cm) of plastic cable conduit.
- 1 × 4ft (1.2m) length of pond pump hose of a diameter that will fit the pump's outlet pipe.
- This project required the creation of a steel, welded stand to enable the standing stone to site safely. It was eventually hidden under the walling material.

Tools

- Spade.
- Shovel.
- Pick or mattock.
- Sledgehammer.
- Bucket.
- Large trowel and pointing trowel.
- Rubber mallet.
- Hacksaw.
- Spirit level.
- Tape measure.

Method

The reservoir is of similar design and shape to the raised pond described earlier, but only half its height and diameter, as it is only going to be a sump for the water that will eventually trickle out from the top of the standing stone. Like the raised pond, the sump walls should sit in a concreted foundation of at least 6in (15cm) in depth. To build the walls, follow the method described for the raised pond, but this time you do not have to create a shallow area, as the reservoir has one depth only. After constructing the penultimate course, skim the entire inside area with mortar and, if possible, sculpture a concaved bowl. Next, line the inner area with damp sand, following the same method described for the raised pond, remembering that there is no requirement for planting shelves. As soon as you have done this, lay the butyl liner and then trim off the excess.

It is now time to place the welded frame

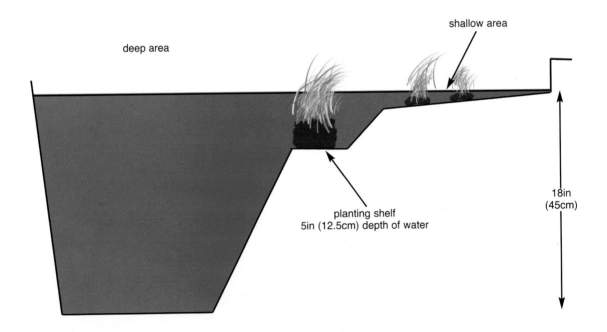

Cross-section of a raised pond showing different water levels.

onto the reservoir walls and lift the standing stone into position. Having done this, insert the pump directly underneath the stone. Push the pond pump hose down the standing stone's bore hole until it appears below, and attach it to the pump's outlet pipe. Trim the hose level with the top of the standing stone. Using the hacksaw, saw down one side of the plastic conduit, then wrap it around the solar cell cable and rest it on the top edge of the reservoir wall. After mixing some more mortar, secure the last course of walling stone, ensuring that the welded frame and plastic conduit are mortared into place also; refer to the raised pond section for instruc-

tions on cementing the top stones to the pond liner.

The next job is to fill the reservoir with water, switch on the pump and adjust the head (water flow) so that it just trickles down the standing stone back into the sump. When you are satisfied that everything is working, place some large random stones over the top of the structure to hide the steel frame. Once you have done this, lay smaller stones or large pebbles over any gaps. It is advisable not to mortar any of this material, as you may need to access the pump for maintenance. To finish, point the walls of the reservoir using the method described for the raised pond.

Pond Plants

Marginals
These plants can be sighted on the pond's shallow planting shelves:

Alisma plantago
Butomus umbellatus
Calla
Caltha palustris
Carex pendula
Carex pseudocyperus
Carex riparia
Cyperus longus
Geum rivale
Iris pseudacorus
Lythrum
Mentha aquatica
Menyanthes
Myosotis scirpoides
Ranunculus lingua grandiflora
Rumex hydrolapathum
Saggitaria saggitifolia
Scirpus lacustris
Scirpus tabernaemontani
Sparganium erectum
Typha angustifolia
Veronica beccabunga

Water Lilies
These plants prefer running water or ponds containing a fountain/waterfall; lilies do not like still water. Use white water lilies to suit the size of the pond. The native water lily Alba is rampant and only suitable for very large ponds; an alternative is Nuphar lutea.

Oxygenators
Oxgenators are ideal for wildlife ponds if a moving water source isn't available to oxygenate the water:

Callitriche
Ceratophyllum
Myriophyllum spicatum
Potamogeton crispus
Ranunculus sp.

Floaters

Hydrocharis
Stratiotes
Ultricularia

Problem Plants
The root stocks of the following plants may damage pond liners:

Phragmites
Scirpus maritimus
Spargatina pectinata
Typha latifolia

Owing to the growth habit of *Elodea* it should not be planted in a natural pond with a soil bottom. *Ceratophyllum* and *Potamogeton crispus* are generally better plants in this situation. *Equisetums*, once planted in a natural condition, are very difficult to control as the roots go very deep.

CHAPTER EIGHT

Small Stone Features

I considered many small features for inclusion in this book. Most objects such as barbecues have already been written about so it seemed pointless reinventing the wheel, as it were. I eventually settled on three garden items that seemed practical, aesthetic and out of the ordinary in design. The first one is a stone seat or bench, constructed from semidressed and random material, the second is a circle of standing stones and the third is simply a random stone planting bed.

STONE CIRCLE

Our stone circle was installed to complement the garden's upper seating area, mainly because the surrounding retaining wall took a circular/horseshoe shape. I also wanted to construct a standing stone waterfall (described in Chapter 7) but the client thought differently of the idea. However, it would have made an ideal central ornament for the stone circle. Standing stones look ancient and mysterious, and were possibly among the first major stone constructions in human history. They can also serve a practical wildlife purpose inasmuch as you can use them as rather effective, natural, bird feeders.

Materials

- Around six or seven tall stones of roughly 2ft (60cm) in height (or taller, if you can handle them).
- Sand and cement.

The foundation for the standing stone filled with mortar.

Installing the standing stone into the mortar.

Smoothing and skimming the mortar around the base of the standing stone.

The completed standing stone; soil has been shovelled in to hide the mortar.

A row of three standing stones on the right-hand side of the seating area.

All standing stones have now been installed. The ladder and planks in the background were our only method of importing stone into the garden.

Tools

- Spade.
- Shovel.
- Large trowel.
- Spirit level.
- Bucket.

Method

Firstly, mark the areas where you want your stones to be sited. The finished project will be more aesthetically pleasing if the stones are equal distances apart. Next, dig a small hole of around 6in (15cm) in depth and to the width of the stone in use. After this, completely fill the hole with mortar and then carefully insert the stone, checking it with the spirit level. When you are satisfied that the stone is level, use the large trowel to smooth and skim the mortar around the standing stone's base. Lastly, cover the mortar with soil and leave to set. Repeat this procedure for the remaining stones.

FIXED STONE BENCH

Every garden needs a seat or two, but most furniture looks out of place next to features made from natural stone; the exception is wrought iron tables and chairs, but these tend to be quite expensive. If you can get hold of around three suitable semi-dressed or dressed stones (stone that has been cut or chiselled into shape), then you have three-quarters of the stone material required to construct your own seat; all you will need in addition is one half of a large flagstone or similar.

Materials

- Three pieces of dressed random stone roughly 1–1.5ft (30–45cm) high and between 6–7in (15–17cm) in width, with a thickness of no less than 3in (7.5cm).
- Sand and cement.

Tools

- Spade.
- Shovel.
- Large trowel.
- Pointing trowel.
- Rubber mallet.
- Spirit level.
- Tape measure.

Method

Choose the site for your bench carefully, because once it is constructed it becomes a permanent fixture and can only be removed if completely dismantled. If you want it set at

The stone seat's plinth, bedded in and pointed. Note the actual large stone seat on the ground.

A generous layer of mortar has been placed on the plinth and is now ready for the seat to be laid on top.

Checking the level of the bench with the spirit level.

The completed stone seat. This is before the large patio was installed, and the seat's height was designed for a child.

The stone seat viewed from the front.

an angle to complement another feature or to enable a special garden view when sitting down, it is best to work it out now. Assuming the site has been earmarked, lay the three dressed stones upright, forming a U shape. From this starting point, mark a foundation trench, using the stones as a template. Next, remove the stones and excavate the foundation to a maximum (not minimum) depth of 6in (15cm). After you have done this, fill the trench with mortar, then place the first stone. Take the large trowel and spread some fresh mortar up the edge of the stone that will form a join with the next one, and then lay the sec-

ond stone into the foundation. Check them with the spirit level and adjust if necessary: the tops of the stones have to be perfectly flush with each other. Repeat the procedure just described for the last stone. You have now created the seat's plinth. Leave this to set for around two hours.

When you are ready to affix the stone flag, spread a thick layer of mortar onto the top of the plinth and carefully lay the flagstone, gently bedding it down with the rubber mallet, checking it with the spirit level at the same time. To complete the bench, point all joins using the method described in Chapter

Raising the height of the stone seat for adult use.

Laying and bedding in some more stone.

The extra course of walling stone has now raised the plinth to adult height.

A generous covering of mortar ready for the large stone to be placed.

7 for the raised pond. Leave to dry and harden for around twenty-four hours before using.

You will notice that project photos depict the stone seat as a low bench and as a higher bench. This was not a mistake; it is an example of a low child's seat and a slightly higher adult's version.

VEGETABLE/PLANTING BED

There is a common misconception that the use of raised beds as a base for growing lessens the amount of space for plants or vegetables. This is not the case: raised beds are 'double dug'. As such, the soil structure allows rootstock to penetrate downward as opposed to outward, allowing for closer planting. Although the initial construction of a raised bed garden can be harder work than, say, the annual digging of rows, once completed there is no real need ever to dig the soil again. Soil fertility and tilth is maintained by the addition of compost every year. There is also no need to stand on a bed as planting can be carried out from the paths, therefore avoiding soil compaction. The soil structure in a bed system is good, moisture is retained and droughts do not pose so great a problem as in conventional gardens. Because it is pos-sible to have plants in greater density than normal, a higher yield can be achieved for a given space. The interconnecting paths, which are automatically shaped because of the bed system, can be surfaced with gravel or bark to prevent erosion.

A raised bed can be any length, but the ideal maximum width is 4ft (1.2m), as this means that planting and maintenance can be carried out whilst standing on the path. A number of raised beds, especially within the vegetable garden, allows for simple rotation of crops and control of soil disease. Beds can even host a number of plants such as runner beans in the middle and catch crops like lettuce or radish down the edges; this is because no soil has to be wasted for paths, thereby making full use of the bed's growing area.

Materials

- Around 1.5 tons of medium to large stone (this will be enough to construct one raised bed).
- At least four small stakes.
- Mulch such as Terram. If you decide to install gravel or bark paths than you will need this underneath for weed control. If

double-dug beds allow for more crops to be planted because root systems penetrate downwards as opposed to sideways

paths wide enough for maintenance including lawn mowers, strimmers and wheelbarrows

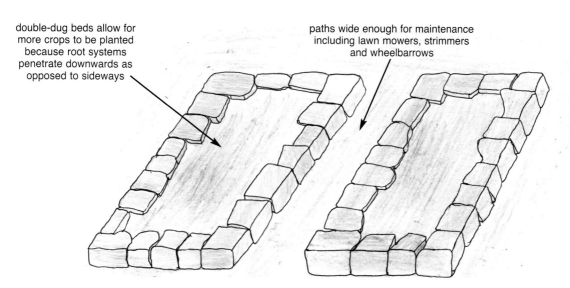

Raised stone beds.

you intend to keep the paths grassy, then the space between each bed must be wide enough for easy strimming or a lawn mower. Paths should be wide enough to allow the transporting of materials via a wheelbarrow anyway.

Tools

- Spade.
- Pick or mattock.
- Garden fork.
- Garden rake.
- Wheelbarrow.
- Spirit level.
- Lump hammer.
- String line.
- Tape measure.

Method

The first job is to plan where you want to situate your beds; this is entirely up to personal choice and dependent on the shape of your plot, so it may be a good idea to draw a simple plan. Once you are satisfied, the work can begin. Start by estimating where the bed's first corner will go, then drive one of the small stakes into the ground with the lump hammer. Next, take the tape measure and measure the chosen length of your bed then drive in a second stake. From this stake, take a width measurement of 4ft (1.2m) and place the third stake; next, measure back down the length to ascertain where the fourth stake should go. Now use the string line to create a rectangular template by attaching it to all four stakes, ensuring it is pulled tight. Working from the outside of the string template, dig a shallow foundation of no more than 4in (10cm) around the entire perimeter, then slightly loosen the foundation's base with the garden fork. You only need to create a 2in (5cm) layer of loose subsoil.

The stones for the bed can now be laid. Start from one end by inserting the first stone, making sure it is firmly bedded into the loose subsoil. Take a second stone and do

the same, but his time abut it tightly to edge of the first. Continue in this fashion until you have created the shell of your raised bed.

Working in the inside of the bed, remove any turf and place to one side, out of the structure's way. Follow these simple instructions for double digging your bed:

1 Dig a trench one spade-length deep (9–10in, 23–25cm) and the length of your planting area.
2 Place the soil in a wheelbarrow.
3 Loosen the soil at the bottom of the trench another 9–10in with the garden fork. You can do this by forcing the prongs into the ground, then moving the rake backward and forward. Shovel some compost into the trench (if your soil requires a conditioner then some old hay, forked into the bottom of the trench, will suffice). Using the fork, thoroughly mix them into the subsoil.
4 Dig a second, parallel, trench using the same method.
5 Use the topsoil from the second trench to fill the first one, adding more organic matter and mixing it in.
6 Repeat this procedure until you have completed the entire bed. Use the soil from the wheelbarrow to fill the last trench.

Maintenance of Your Double-Dug Bed

Usually the soil structure within a double-dug bed remains healthy, but during the first two years some compaction may occur. Compaction is caused by rainfall or watering, and if this does occur all you will have to do during the winter is loosen the topsoil with a garden fork, ensuring not to dig it in. Essential soil bacteria exist within the first 2in (5cm) of soil, so burying this will only cause harm. Soil compaction will soon disappear once you have created a healthy and fine loam. There should be no need to re-dig the bed and compost can be shovelled on to the top, during the winter months. Frost and earthworm action will then do all the work for you.

CHAPTER NINE

Stone Steps

A flight of stone steps offers a durable, long-lasting alternative to wooden steps and to the soil/grass ramps that will quickly erode into muddy quagmires. It is a good idea to install steps on any garden access point that leads to higher ground or a terrace. The stone size available will dictate whether you will need to bed the steps into mortar. Large stone flags, for example, have a surface area and shape sufficient enough for them to be placed on granular soil and on top of each other, then left dry. Smaller stones should be bonded with sand and cement, otherwise they become unstable and dangerous.

There are varying techniques associated with differing sizes of stone. Some call for the laying of a mortar base, others are built in the same fashion as a wet stone wall, the more interesting ones are 'stone pitched', but the strongest are laid using large, stone slabs where their weight – apart from the odd securing wedge – holds them firmly in position. Stone size will largely depend on the availability of supply and budget. There is an adage that 'if it requires two people to manoeuvre a stone, it won't move when one person walks on it'. That statement is more accurate when you add '... if it's correctly set into the ground'.

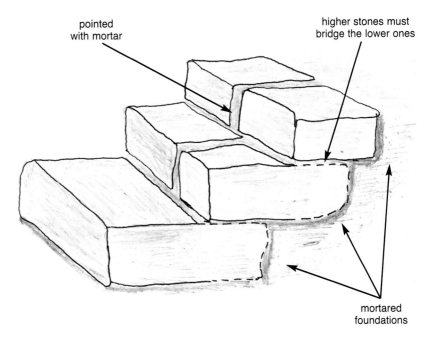

pointed with mortar

higher stones must bridge the lower ones

mortared foundations

Stone steps.

A small flight of stone steps, similar to the ones described, leading into a wildlife garden.

Materials

- Around 1 ton of indigenous, random stone per square metre. The quantity is only a guide and an overestimate, for the simple reason that various sections of terrain used more stone than others on the route.
- Sand and cement.
- Plasticizer. For winter tasks you can use a solution that includes an antifreeze.

Tools

- Spade.
- Crowbar.
- Pick.
- Mattock.
- Shovel.
- Rubber maul for bedding in large stone.
- Lump hammer for bedding in smaller stone.
- Bucket, handy for storing mixed mortar, hearting stones and pinning.
- String line.
- Pointing trowel.
- Wheelbarrow for transporting materials around the site. Can be used as a receptacle for mixing sand and cement.
- Powered cement mixer. This is obviously the preferred cement-mixing tool.

An example of stone steps using various courses of walling stone.

BUILDING STONE RISERS

This project assumes a bottom step made from two large sections of random stone. Step construction tasks must start from the bottom of the slope. This is more crucial when building in stone because, in all cases, the lower step relies on the higher one to help firming.

Begin by excavating a foundation trench down to a firm sub-soil structure in order to support the heavy stone that is going to be laid on top. Digging to a depth of around 6in (15cm) usually suffices, but in waterlogged soils you may have to unearth more spoil.

Having dug the trench, the base should be inspected for soft areas; tamping in medium-to small-sized rocks can firm these up.

Shovel a generous layer of mortar into the concrete foundation. Before you begin always fill a bucket with pinning and place it at arm's length. Next, search for a stone with a decent length; ideally, it should have a smooth top and underside, but it will more than likely be a wedge shape. If that's the case, turn the smooth side uppermost and bed the angled side into the mortar, with its face touching the front edge side of the trench. Taking the rubber mallet, gently tap the stone downward until the mortar starts to

Building mortared stone steps.

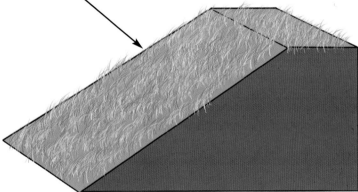

a path that climbs a grassy slope will soon erode and become a muddy hazard during the winter

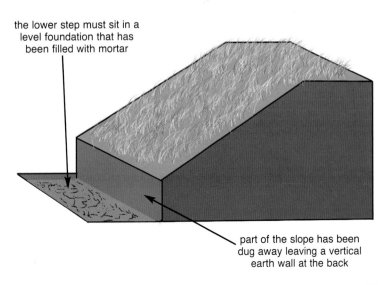

the lower step must sit in a level foundation that has been filled with mortar

part of the slope has been dug away leaving a vertical earth wall at the back

Laying the first step (1).

the first step should be bedded
into the mortared foundation and
levelled using a spirit level

Laying the first step (2).

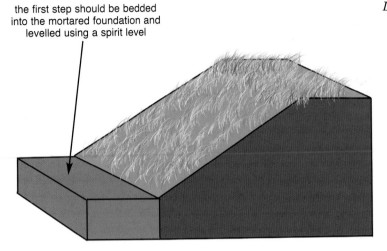

ooze from all sides. The top of the stone has to be level for the second step. If it is seems to be sloping downward, carefully lift it and insert pinning from behind, then pack it with as much small stone and cement as you can. Using the trowel, skim the oozed-out cement up the side of the stone, gently forcing it around the pinners.

Next, trowel a quantity of fresh mortar up the side of the stone in preparation for the next one. Lay a second stone, of similar height, on the foundation and abut it to the first, then bed it down with the rubber mallet. You may have to brace the first stone with your free hand in case it is pushed out of alignment. Use the spirit level to check the levels of the two stones, and adjust them if required. Point the joins with fresh mortar, using the method described in Chapter 7 for the raised pond.

The Second Step

The next phase of the project adds a second, higher step to first one. First off, excavate another foundation; this will have to be level with the top (or platform) of the lower tread. The second step has to be large enough in order to bridge the one below. Bridging the

the slope should be excavated
level with the top of the lower step

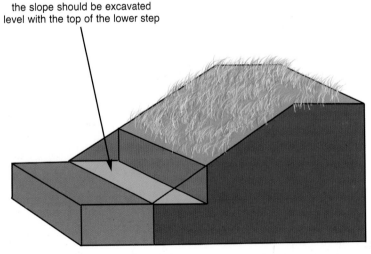

Laying the second step (1).

Laying the second step (2).

after excavating the slope for
the second step, lay a thick bed
of mortar on the foundation
ensuring that it covers the step
below by at least 5in (12.5cm)

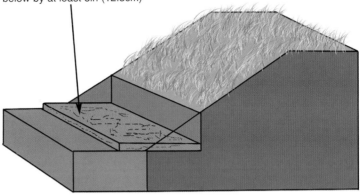

if you have to use more than one stone
to create a step, make sure that their
lengths are running toward the slope –
this will create a secure walking platform

all joins
must be
mortared

Laying the second step (3).

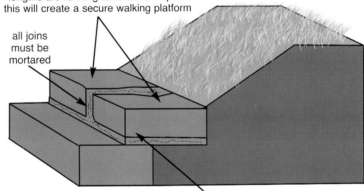

at least 5in (12.5cm)of the higher
step must rest on the lower step

the remaining steps are constructed
using the same method as for the
first and second steps

all mortared
joints must be
bridged by the
higher step

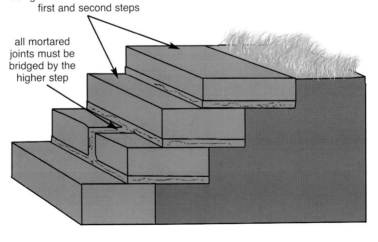

Building to the top of the slope.

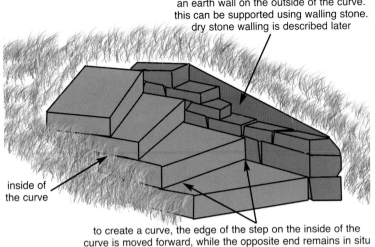

an earth wall on the outside of the curve. *Adding curves to stone steps.*
this can be supported using walling stone.
dry stone walling is described later

inside of
the curve

to create a curve, the edge of the step on the inside of the
curve is moved forward, while the opposite end remains in situ

two steps is an essential structural feature, because they then become solid and act as one structure. Apart from bridging, another important structural feature is to stagger the joins of the lower step. For example, if the lower step is made up of two or three stones – creating joins – then the higher step must cross these joins.

To lay the second step, shovel a generous layer of mortar onto the back of the first one, ensuring an even covering of both foundation and lower step. The second step must bridge the lower one by a minimum of 5in (7.5cm) or a quarter of its depth, depending on which is more feasible. Create the second step using the same method as the first. Continue building steps until level ground on the upper section of the slope has been reached. Point up all steps using the technique described in Chapter 7.

STONE FLAG STEPS

Materials
Enough flagstones to create your steps. This will be dependent on the size of slope, but as a guide, each riser will only raise the height by around 2in (5cm).

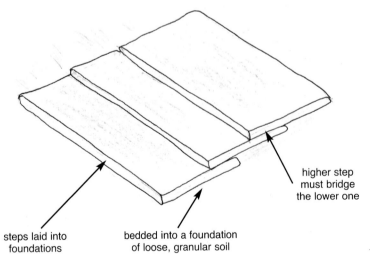

steps laid into
foundations

bedded into a foundation
of loose, granular soil

higher step
must bridge
the lower one

Flagstone steps.

Flagstone steps.

Tools

- Spade.
- Pick or mattock.
- Garden fork.
- Spirit level.
- Tape measure.
- Large rubber maul.

Method

Although cumbersome and heavy to manoeuvre around the work site, stone flags make excellent steps as they are very stable due to their vast surface area. It is, however, a job for more than one person and it may even take three or four individuals to safely lift them into position. The main benefit with this style of construction is the fact that it does not require the use of mortar as a bedding mixture. Stone flags will comfortably sit in a shallow foundation of granular soil. The construction technique is basically the same as any other step-building task.

Each flag must sit in a level foundation, but the depth need only be around 3in (7.5cm) maximum. Having excavated this foundation, the subsoil must be loosened with either a spade or garden fork. A flag will require at least 2in (5cm) of loose soil for bedding down.

Once the foundation for the first step has been created, the initial flag can be moved into place. As I explained earlier, this is usually a task for more than one person. When the step is in position, bed it down with the rubber maul, then check its level with the spirit level. On rare occasions stone flags, if they wobble, may require additional wedges inserted from behind. This won't pose much of a problem, for the second flag's weight, when bridged with the lower one, will secure it in place.

The second flagstone, and all remanding stones, are laid in exactly the same fashion, but you must ensure that each one bridges the lower step by at least 5in (12.5cm).

CHAPTER TEN

Dry Stone and Wet Stone Retaining Walls

There are two basic styles of natural stone walls, dry stone walls and wet stone walls. Regardless of the style of wall you are building, it is a good idea to understand the fundamental principles behind the dry stone walling technique, as both rely on the same features, the only difference being the wet stone version also uses mortar, whilst its dry stone cousin does not. Dry stone walls are hard-wearing and long-lasting. If one raises a wet stone wall using as much of this technique as possible, your completed feature should be strong enough to withstand the rigours of nature and time.

DOUBLE-SKINNED WALLS

This wall comprises of two sides, which face out, and is built in a succession of interlocked layers or 'courses'. Large foundation stones help to provide a secure base for the rest of the outer stones, called face-stones, which are gradually laid in single courses to form a wall. Wet and dry natural stone walls are built to form an apex. This is called the slope or 'batter'. The batter serves two purposes: it helps to disperse the weight evenly toward the ground; and it ensures that any movement, natural or otherwise, is forced toward the centre of the structure. In effect, the two sides are leaning against each other.

The batter is achieved by using a device called a batter frame. This is comprised of two wooden structures that represent the width and height of the desired wall. They are secured at each end of the proposed wall, connected to one another by string lines. The string lines represent the wall's outer faces and are used as a template when laying face-stones. The use of the batter frame and string lines enables the waller to erect a feature free of bulges and serious irregularities; this is achieved by making sure that the front of a face-stone is laid in parallel alignment with the string.

As each stone is placed or laid on the wall, it is strengthened from behind with small pieces of rubble called wedges, pinning or pinning stone. These are small wedge-shaped pieces of stone pushed under the gaps at the back of each face-stone to secure it to the wall without wobbling. Random stone is unstable; even placed on a flat surface it will wobble. Strategically placed pinning will counter any movement like this. Pinning is essential in a mortared wall also. The reason for this is down to the random shape of the building material. Large amounts of mortar will eventually begin to break down due to weathering; so as much of the area underneath the back of the stone should be bolstered with smaller materials. The safest method is to insert the pinning stone to counter movement, then force mortar into the remaining gaps.

As the stones are laid and pinned, gaps will appear in the wall's centre. These holes are filled with more rubble, called hearting-stone. For wet stone walls, use an equal quantity of mortar and stone to fill the wall's central areas. Whenever possible, face-stones are placed with their entire length into the wall, resting on the hearting or mortar/hearting mix. This helps to tie the face-stones to the centre of the wall, to bind both sides of the wall together in fact.

Another method of using throughs is to place them on a single layer, halfway up the wall. The top layer of wall is called the coping. Coping stones bridge the two skins of wall and are tightly locked together to form a rigid course. The top of a wall is built out of smaller material; the use of coping ensures that these thinner, weaker courses are securely tied together. A wall without coping is a prime candidate for decay. The heart of the wall will be susceptible to weather erosion and its supporting face-stones easily pushed off by livestock or people. Laying coping stones vertically, with their thinnest part on the wall, means that more material can be used, therefore creating as much weight as possible to disperse throughout the entire structure. Wet stone walls do not require vertical coping and top stones can be laid with their wider surface areas to the wall, then pointed up.

A few styles require the coping to be laid horizontally (the greater surface area placed on the wall). Retaining walls are constructed this way. In this case it is the heaviest, flattest stones, which are used in such a manner that they tie the top of the wall to the soil bank.

Just as the top of a wall is sealed by the coping, the end of the wall has to be secured also, and this is the same for wet stone walls. This is accomplished by building wall-ends or cheek-ends. These sections are incorporated into each course as the wall gains in height. End-stones should be long enough to span the width of any given course and are laid using a 2-on-1 or 1-on-2 technique. '1' is a through stone placed across the wall's width. '2' are similar sized stones, called runners, which

literally run down the line of each of the wall's faces, tying the through-stones to the main body of wall. A further through-stone is laid on the runners and so it continues until the wall reaches coping height.

In the case of the dry stone wall, each stone – including hearting and pinning – is an independent object, yet they all serve one purpose, to stop the wall from falling down. Wet stone walls will become one rigid object.

DRY STONE RETAINING WALL

Retaining walls are used primarily for supporting unstable soil banks, which otherwise may subside due the effect of erosion. The height of this style of wall is governed by the size of soil bank behind and could range from as little as 1ft (30cm) to as much as 10ft (3m) and higher. Out of all the walling styles this is probably the most popular, especially with the enthusiastic gardener, as it can be used to create ornamental garden features. On average, there are more retaining dry stone walls built than any other style. This is down to the fact that this style of wall is a very popular garden ornament.

The construction principles remain the same for this wall as it does for a double-skinned wall: laying large stones at the base, building even courses of pinned face-stone, erecting strong wall-ends and finishing with a row of coping. All retaining walls, without exception, have to be built with a batter. Without this, any movement of the soil structure behind could push the wall over. The major role of the batter is to help counter the force of the soil bank on the wall by spreading this energy through each face-stone before it is released at the foundation course.

Basic Techniques

To the uninitiated, building a dry stone wall using just random stone can appear daunting, and forming a long-lasting, solid structure from such material, virtually impossible. The most important ingredients in the craft are understanding what to look for in the stone and knowing where and how to lay it on the wall. This is not some mysterious technique that only the walling or stonemason community is able to comprehend, but comes with hands-on experience. Some people can grasp it straight away, after the first few courses of face-stone. For others it can take a little longer, but not as long as learning to drive, for instance.

When searching for face-stone, the experienced dry stone waller automatically asks him or herself a number of important questions, not necessarily in the following order:

1 Does it have a vertical side that can face out from the wall? Believe it or not, almost all random stone has an aesthetic edge, which can face out from the wall. Ideally, the waller looks for a face that is slightly angled away from the wall; this helps to deflect rainwater from the centre.
2 Can the next course be built on top of it? If the top of the stone is too angular with hardly any flat surface area, then there is a possibility that the stone above will move, even when the wall is complete.
3 Will it leave enough room for the stone that is going to be laid on the other side of the wall? If the face-stone is laid, but only leaves just 1 or 2 inches of room for the stone on the neighbouring side, then this part of the wall could become unstable when the wall settles. This is called 'walling out'.

The face-stones create the wall's batter and aesthetic appearance, and it is vitally important that each one is laid following the basic principles. Any mistakes now may not become apparent until after the wall settles, by when it will be too late to rectify them. Dry stone walls are not just built using strength and physical activity; the process requires an immense amount of concentration and thought. If, at any time during construction, concentration wanes and one becomes totally bogged down and unable to select the right stone, do not panic! It happens to the best and

most experienced. The only way get around this problem is to take a break and think about something completely different. Upon returning to the task the answer is invariably there waiting.

Materials

- Half of a ton of stone for each square metre (9sq ft) of retaining wall; this includes material for coping, hearting and pinning.

Tools

- Crowbar.
- Pick or mattock.
- Spade.
- Walling hammer or lump hammer.
- Rake.

Safety Equipment

- Steel toe protectors.
- Eye protectors.
- Leather working gloves. (Natural stone can be abrasive or sharp, so rubber safety gloves will shred with hours.)

Method

The first step is to prepare a footing. A footing is essentially a foundation that establishes a base for the wall and, at the same time, shows where the front wall face will be. You can mark the foundation's outline by using a spade. Next, excavate the soil to a depth of 6in (15cm), or until you reach firm, granular subsoil, and about 8in (20cm) wide. Both the depth and the width of the footing depend largely on the height of the wall.

Before construction, it is necessary to insert batter-rods at either end of the proposed wall. Usually, small lengths of retaining wall only require two, one at either end. Where a long section of wall is to be constructed, a third rod can be inserted halfway between the two to stop the string line from sagging. Hammer the rods into the ground with a lump hammer, at the same time adjusting them for the batter. The angle can be anything from 1 in 4 to 1 in 6.

Tie an end of the string-line to one of the rods, about 2in (5cm) off the ground, then tie the other end to the next rod, pulling it as tight as possible, at the same height. As with a double-skinned dry stone wall, the batter of a retaining wall is important. To ensure an even slope, a second string-line can be tied to the top of the rods. To inspect the batter, stand behind one of the rods and look directly down the string lines. If the two strings are travelling in different directions, one appearing to go left and the other to the right, the batter is wrong. Correct it by adjusting the

angles of the rods until the strings run a parallel course.

Lay the end-stones first. They must project into the bank, sealing the ends of the course. Align the front of the stone so that it runs parallel and just touches the string. Try not to push the string line out of alignment. Lay the remaining foundation stones in the trench with their lengths projecting toward the bank. Abut the sides of each stone together, minimizing the gaps between the joins. Finish the course by inserting hearting behind the stones.

Begin the next course by raising the string line 3–4in (7–10cm) on the batter-rods, then

Prepared soil bank and foundation of a retaining wall.

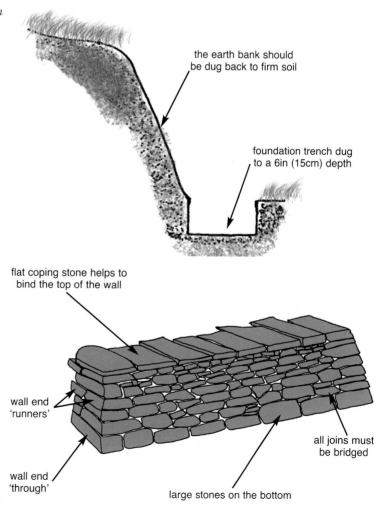

the earth bank should be dug back to firm soil

foundation trench dug to a 6in (15cm) depth

flat coping stone helps to bind the top of the wall

wall end 'runners'

wall end 'through'

large stones on the bottom

all joins must be bridged

Single-skinned, dry stone retaining wall.

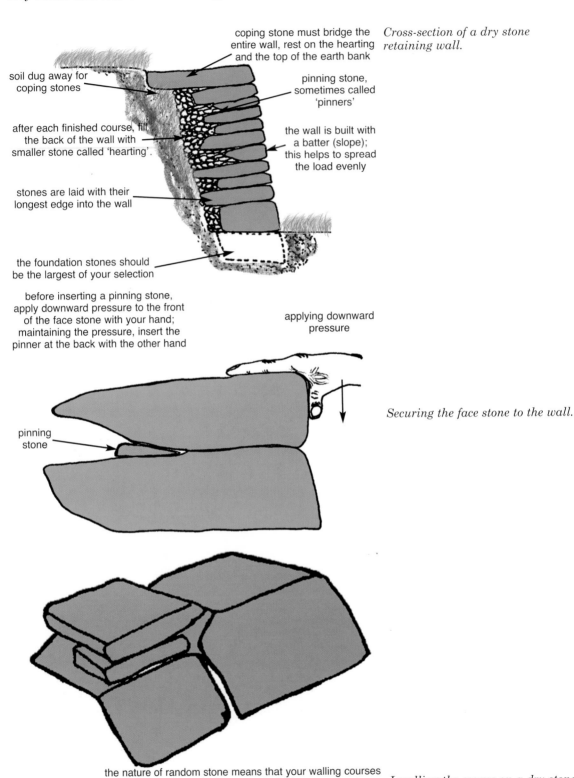

coping stone must bridge the entire wall, rest on the hearting and the top of the earth bank

Cross-section of a dry stone retaining wall.

soil dug away for coping stones

pinning stone, sometimes called 'pinners'

after each finished course, fill the back of the wall with smaller stone called 'hearting'.

the wall is built with a batter (slope); this helps to spread the load evenly

stones are laid with their longest edge into the wall

the foundation stones should be the largest of your selection

before inserting a pinning stone, apply downward pressure to the front of the face stone with your hand; maintaining the pressure, insert the pinner at the back with the other hand

applying downward pressure

Securing the face stone to the wall.

pinning stone

the nature of random stone means that your walling courses will not be level; to enable you to build the course on top, smaller stones can be used to raise the lower course

Levelling the course on a dry stone wall.

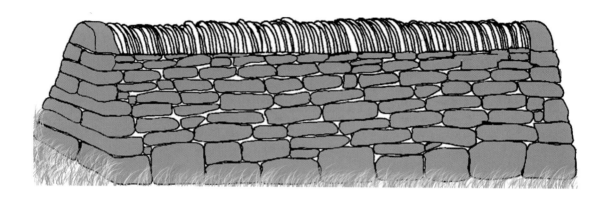

Double-skinned dry stone wall.

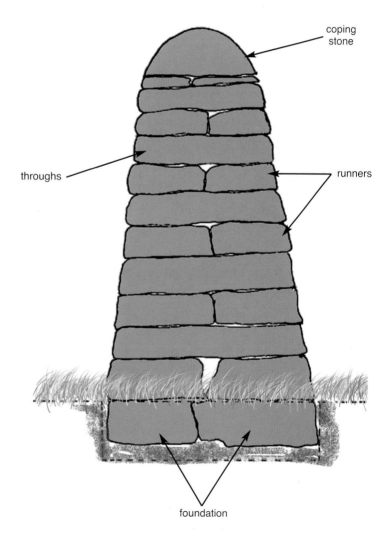

coping
stone

throughs

runners

foundation

*Wall-end of a double-skinned dry
stone wall.*

lift the next end-stones on the wall. Wall-ends on a retaining wall are built in exactly the same way as on a double-skinned wall, using the same pattern of alternate throughs and runners. The only difference is that the runners at the back of the wall bridge over to the hearting as opposed to the second skin. Through-stones should be laid so the back is inserted into the bank or, at least, touching it.

Build the next course of face-stones, inserting pinners when needed and adjusting their fronts in accordance with the string line. Back-fill with hearting, taking care not to disturb the pinning stone. Continue in the same fashion until half of the wall is constructed; this will be the height of the through-band.

The through-band on a retaining wall is designed to bind the lower half of wall to the soil bank. Through-stones are laid on the course, then literally dug into the soil. The wall, in effect, then becomes part of the bank.

Once the through-band is secured, the rest of the course can be brought level. Small retaining walls will not require a through-band. Build the remaining courses to just below the level of the soil bank, using the method just described. The reason for this is that the top of the soil bank will need to be dug away to produce a level area for the coping to sit on. This helps to minimize the scope for future movement of the stones.

The Coping-Stones

Although there are some styles of retaining wall that host a vertical coping, on walls that may be climbed over or sat on, the coping is best laid with its greater surface area to the wall. A flat stone will even out any weight that could be applied if the wall is walked on, consequently protecting the courses below.

Before laying the coping, move the string line to lie 1in (2.5cm) above the top of the wall. Using this line as a guide, lay the cop-

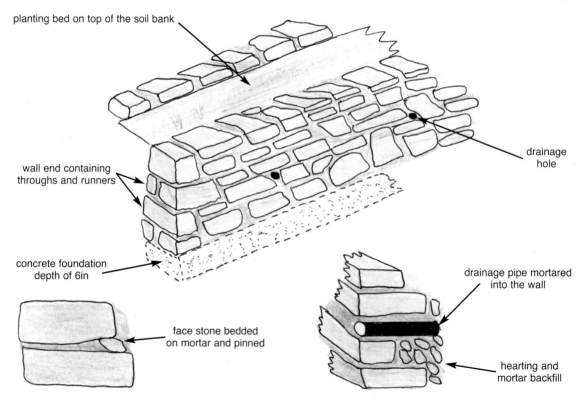

A wet stone retaining wall.

ing-stones so that their tops just brush the string. Adjust the stones until their fronts are parallel with the rest of the wall. Raise the height of any coping stone that appears angled along the front face by inserting a thin face-stone underneath to bring it level. The small stone will, of course, need pinning and the gaps created underneath the coping should be filled with small hearting.

Finally, finish the wall by ramming in soil or turf between the gaps of the coping on the soil bank. Refrain from doing this on the wall as it may unsettle the stones below. If you have a planting area behind the wall, brush soil into all gaps and rake level with the top of the wall, Eventually, when the vegetation or plants begin to grow they will help to bond the coping-stones together.

Suitable Plants
Most alpine varieties will grow easily on the top of the wall (wet or dry stone) or in the wall's gaps between bridging joins (dry stone wall only).

WET STONE RETAINING WALL

The same building technique is used for this style as for the one constructed out of dry stone. The difference is that mortar is used as well as hearting and pinning, and the front of the construction is pointed.

BUILDING A FREE-STANDING DRY STONE WALL

The primary role of dry stone walls in the UK is stock enclosure, but they also appear in gardens as ornamental features. In most upland regions in Britain, such as the Lake District and Peak District National Parks, dry stone walls are common garden boundaries and their repair and maintenance in these regions is as common as looking after garden fencing in towns and cities. The majority of dry stone walls are built to 4½ft (1.5m), but this basic dimension can vary due to the size and quality of local stone. In the

Cotswolds, for example, the individual portions of stone are too small and most walls there only reach around 3ft (1m) in height.

The width of the wall is dependent on its finished height. The distance across the base should be half the height, and the width at the top should be half the width of the bottom. This will mean that a wall of 4ft 6in (1.4m) in height will be 2ft 3in (68cm) wide at foundation level and around 14in (36cm) wide where the coping should go. It does not matter what region a dry stone wall is built in, its construction will follow a set of basic procedures. These are important techniques and, if used successfully, will ensure the finished, durable feature.

As mentioned earlier most quarries in upland Britain cater for the dry stone walling community and ordering a load of stone from these places should not pose much of a problem. In lowland areas, however, this may prove slightly more difficult and so I have included a list of contacts at the back of this book. Regardless of how the stone is brought in, you will find that when it arrives on site the pile will be a mixture of small, medium and large materials. The first job is to separate large stones for use as foundations, throughs and end stones, then organize material that will be ideal for the coping and, finally, separate out small and medium items for use as face-stones, hearting and pinning.

Materials

- 1 ton of random walling stone for every 3ft (1m) of wall constructed to a height of 4ft (1.2m).

Tools

- Walling hammer or lump hammer.
- Bolster chisel.
- Sledgehammer.
- Spade.
- Wheelbarrow.
- Bucket.

- Crowbar (for moving large stone around the site or for aiding the removal of large materials when excavating the wall's foundation).
- String line.
- Tape measure.
- Batter rods or a batter frame.

Method

Before construction begins there are a few basic and important elements of this craft to consider. They are as follows:

- Keep a safe working distance between the unused stone and the wall under construction.
- Use the largest stones for the foundation course and bottom courses, gradually building in order of decreasing size on higher courses.
- Every stone, where possible, should be placed with its length toward the centre of the wall. Stone set the other way could fall away when the wall settles.
- The stone should sit on the course horizontally or with its back slightly raised. This will deflect rainwater from the important heart (centre) of the wall.
- Insert pinners under each stone when it is placed on the wall. Use as much pinning stone as required until the stone in question sits firm. Avoid inserting pinners into the wall's outer face, because when the wall settles these will come adrift. Small mammals and birds, such as voles and wrens, may push them out also.
- The majority of walling styles require their centres to be filled with hearting stone. When filling the wall with hearting it is important to be careful not to disturb the pinners under the face-stones.
- Always build one course of wall before starting on the next. On some projects this is not possible, and it may be necessary to build a small section of wall to coping height. Use this method if it is a repair of an existing structure that cannot be finished in one day and stock-proofing is

essential. If you have to do this the courses of the wall should be left stepped, ready to tie in the rest of the wall.
- Cross the joins of each stone on every course. Never allow a join to run on more than two courses high, and try to avoid even this if possible.
- Never drop a stone onto a wall; it will unsettle the courses below. Lay the stone gently on top of another and enlist the aid of another person if it is too heavy to lift.

Creating the Wall's Foundation

The foundation is the most vital section of any heavy building; dry stone walls are no exception. Considering that 1 metre of wall can contain at least 1 ton of stone, whatever is responsible for keeping it up in the years to come will have to be reliable and strong. No matter how well the face-stones are laid, if the foundations are weak it will eventually collapse on itself. A firm foundation course is created by using large stones that require little or no pinning, sitting in a trench of suitable depth and containing a firm, granular subsoil or bedrock base. If the foundation stones are such that they require pinning, these pinners will be pushed further into the ground as the wall settles, forcing the centre of the wall downward. This will probably produce a shift in material on the upper courses, dislodging additional pinning and hearting until the wall eventually falls down.

An obvious recipe for disaster is a foundation course resting on the surface of the soil. Stones will be pushed into the ground and, if the area has a high water table, during the winter the whole construction may sink, be it a small amount, but that will be enough to create unstable courses. A correctly excavated foundation trench, with vertical sides, will prevent this type of damage.

Creating the correct foundation trench is vitally important and can involve many hours of back-breaking work, particularly if the ground is rocky or laden with compacted debris. Woody stemmed plants such as dock or nettle on the proposed line of the wall must be removed, along with their root systems. If they are allowed to grow back through the finished wall, they can dislodge hearting-stones and pinning.

To begin the trench, measure and mark out the area to be excavated. If you have existing garden walls, use their bottom width as a guide; this will ensure that the new wall will match the existing ones. Working from one end of the proposed foundation, use a tape measure to determine accurately the intended width of the trench, then insert two stakes into the ground to mark each of the outer corners. Repeat this at the other end of the wall.

Now you must create a digging template. Do this by tying the string lines to the two stakes at one of the ends, then run them out, just above ground level, to the stakes at the other end. Pulling them tight, tie the strings onto these stakes, making sure that both lines are running parallel.

Work down the outside of the strings with the spade, pushing it vertically into the ground as far as it will go until the foundation's length and width have been clearly marked. Working along the inside of the lines, excavate the trench, keeping the edges vertical, until a firm subsoil or bedrock is reached. This can be anything from 6in (15cm) to a maximum of 12in (30cm), depending on the soil structure. When excavation is complete, flatten the base as much as possible by walking up and down the trench to even out any slopes and undulations. Ramming small stones in with a sledgehammer can firm soft areas up.

The trench is now ready to hold the foundation stones. The first feature to be laid will be the initial stones for both wall-ends. These can either be throughs (stones that span the entire width of the trench) or runners (stones laid on each side of the trench, following the line of the wall). Once the first elements of the wall-ends are settled in, the rest of the foundation course can be constructed. Some of these stones can be very heavy and may require two people to manoeuvre them into the trench. It is for this reason that it is

sound practice to ascertain how they will sit in the trench before lifting them into place. This will avoid major adjustments that may possibly crush the trench sides or gouge deeper into the trench's base. You should identify the largest and flattest surface of the stone, roll the stone over so that this section is facing down, and then move it into the foundation.

Whenever possible, lay the stones so that their lengths run into the centre, but avoid the situation where one cannot be placed on the opposite side. If this happens, either find a shorter stone or, as a last resort, lay the existing one down the length of the trench.

The best foundations are laid below the depth of the topsoil, but the nature of the material will mean some may rise above the trench; this is unavoidable. As soon as a stone is laid a series of fine adjustments can be made to ensure that it is abutted tightly to its neighbouring stones and that the face is running parallel with the edge of the foundation excavation.

When the last foundation stone is securely set, fill the centre of the whole course with large pieces of hearting, taking time to fill all the gaps under each stone. The top of the course should be as level as possible, so ensure the hearting remains flush with the surface. You can test the foundations by applying downward pressure with both hands, gently rocking the stones from side to side, backward and forward. If any stone shows signs of excessive movement, it will need to be reset.

Batter Frames and Batter Rods

There are number of ways to set up the batter frames. Securing them to two stakes at either end of the wall is one option, but this may not work on bedrock. Adding a prop at the back of each frame is an alternative. The most common method, though, is to attach guidelines to the top of the frames and fasten them to the ground with wooden or metal pegs. Some wallers prefer to use metal rods, which are less cumbersome and can be insert-

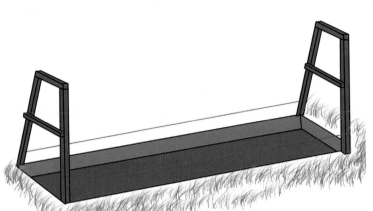

Setting up batter frames with string lines attached.

wall end stone
laid as a through

wall end stone laid
as a two runners

hearting

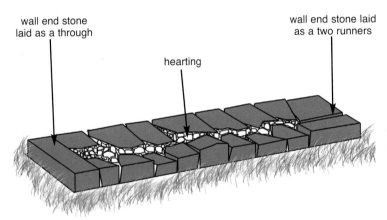

The foundation of the dry stone wall.

the majority of face stones on the lower section of the wall should
be the larger of your selection, but do not use material that can
be utilized as essential throughs, runners and coping stone

all stone must be pinned and hearting
placed between the two faces

wall end –
through stone
laid across
runners

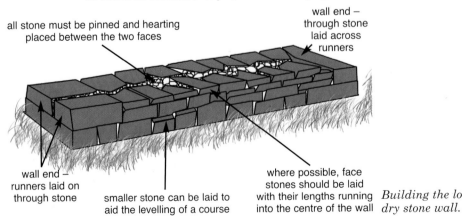

wall end –
runners laid on
through stone

smaller stone can be laid to
aid the levelling of a course

where possible, face
stones should be laid
with their lengths running
into the centre of the wall

Building the lower section of the dry stone wall.

ed into the ground. The way the frames are set up is ultimately a matter of personal preference: the important issue here is to produce the right batter for the wall.

Having successfully secured the frames, attach the string lines for the face-stones. The lines should be tied to the frames at both ends of the wall and no more than 5in (12cm) above the lowest foundation stone. They must be tensioned to reduce any slack, and the width between them as they run parallel down either side of the wall should be equal.

It is likely that the average gardener will not own a set of batter frames, as these tend to be specialist equipment. A set of four 4ft (1.2m) steel rods (or similar) can actually do the same job. If you have existing walls all you would need to do is measure their width at ground level and measure the width of the course of stone before the coping. You can then transfer these dimensions to the new wall by securing the rods into the ground

accordingly. Like the four stakes, which aided the creation of the foundations, these rods are hammered into the corners.

Laying Stones for the Wall-Ends
The first face-stones to be laid on any new course of wall should be the ones for both the wall-ends. This method ensures that the end-stones, which need to be firm and long, are laid on to the course utilizing as much room as required. If a wall-end were to be laid last, then the face-stone on the course may impede an essential through or runner.

Wall-ends are best described as independently constructed pillars, acting like book-ends that secure the face-stone, hearing and pinning in between. They should be built at the start and finish of every dry stone wall, and when there is break for an access point such as a garden gate. Their primary role is to protect the wall from damage by livestock, pets, people and weather. It is for this reason

The completed wall end. Note the vertical coping stone and the large coping on the end of the wall.

Building up a wall end using throughs and runners.

that the stone should be smooth, large and, if possible, rectangular to allow them to be laid without needing to be pinned.

Once the end stones are in place, finish the course of wall by building the first two skins of face-stones between them, bringing their height as level as possible with the tops of the end-stones. Depending on the initial stones, start the next course by using either throughs or runners (if throughs were used on the foundation then use runners on the first

course, or vice versa). Again, build up the two skins of face-stone in between. Repeat this procedure, alternating throughs and runners at the wall ends, until the course is finished.

There are some important points to bear in mind during this procedure. Keep the wall-ends vertical at all times, checking them with a spirit level as the courses go on. Take care not to use small hearting stones between runners, as they will fall away from the end of the wall. On occasion, the width of the runners may not be ideal for the base of the wall, leaving too wide a gap. If there is no large stone available, use three or four runners instead of two.

Face-Stones for the Lower Courses
It is much easier to build stone courses whilst looking directly at the walling face under construction. Large face-stones can be placed on the course without having to drag them from one side of the wall to the other, which will disturb the face-stones already in situ. Always work from one wall-end to the next, building both skins at the same time before starting on the course above. It is easier to lay a row of face-stones on one side of the wall then cross over to work on the opposite skin. However, as the wall gains in height, this becomes increasingly difficult. Experienced craftsmen have mastered the technique of building two skins from one side, but this comes with years of experience; for a novice,

it is not really recommended as the far face cannot be laid accurately or straight. If there is a nearby access point, it will not be too difficult to work from alternate sides. If access is restricted, the only alternative is to carefully scale the wall, resetting any stone disturbed during the process.

The first course of face-stone should, if possible, consist of the largest material available. They must be carefully laid on top of the foundations, abutting the sides of each one together and bridging the joins of the course below. The back of the stone, when resting in its final position on the wall, should be 1mm higher than the face to aid rainwater run-off. Stones that tilt toward the centre will be pushed down even further as the wall settles and they will direct water over hearting and pinning, which will eventually cause erosion. Once in position, turn the face-stone until the front is parallel with the string line. Test the stone for stability by applying downward

Build the two skins of face-stone. Ensure that the stone's length is running into the wall's centre. Note the through stone toward the back of the photograph.

Wall end construction. Note the walling hammer in the centre of the image.

pressure on the front with one hand, rocking it from side to side, backward and forward. If movement is detected during this test, the stone will require pinning to help firm it up. Insert these from behind with the other hand whilst still applying the same downward pressure.

It is important during this phase of construction to ensure that the wall is as level as possible to enable the course above to be laid securely. Due to the nature of random walling this cannot always be achieved by placing just one stone. On many occasions, a few of the stones on the lower level will vary in their height. The only way to solve this problem, if a suitably sized stone cannot be sourced, is to build up the level with smaller face-stones. Even if the top of a stone appears rounded, try to lay it with its widest and flattest side touching the course below. This will ensure that it will fit on the wall with the minimum amount of movement.

The properties of random stone will dictate that sometime during the walling procedure awkward, concave joins will appear and they will need to be bridged by the course above. This rarely occurs when building with sandstone or slate, but is very common on walls constructed with limestone or hard granite. Rather than just lay stones across these large gaps, leaving unsightly triangular gaps, search for suitable candidates to closely match the shape required for the space. It is acceptable for this material to be smaller and thinner than the stones already in place, but they still have to be long enough to penetrate toward the centre of the wall, otherwise all you would be installing is another pinning stone and this, in time, will fall out.

Walling on the Opposite Course
Laying one skin of a course of stone is relatively straightforward because the face-stone penetrates the wall's centre without too much trouble. The opposite side can prove trickier, often requiring specifically sized materials due to the length of the existing material on the wall. This situation applies particularly to the top courses, where room becomes a premium because of the batter. This problem can, however, occur lower down as well. To overcome it, the face-stone is trimmed to size with the chisel end of the walling hammer. It is quite a simple task, which does not require exact accuracy. Simply judge the size needed by placing the face-stone on the wall and estimating how much you will need to cut off, or mark it out with a tape measure and score a line with the bolster chisel, highlighting the amount to trimmed. Lift the stone off the wall and place it on level ground before cutting. Avoid working the front of the stone, because this could create an uneven face.

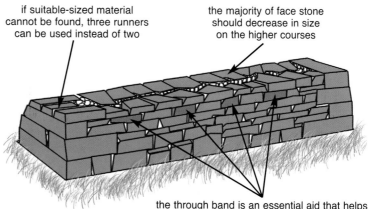

if suitable-sized material cannot be found, three runners can be used instead of two

the majority of face stone should decrease in size on the higher courses

the through band is an essential aid that helps to disperse the weight burden caused by the walling material on the higher courses; throughs must bridge the two faces of the wall

The through-band and the middle section of the wall.

as the wall is built higher,
where possible, smaller
face stone must be laid

Building the higher courses of the wall.

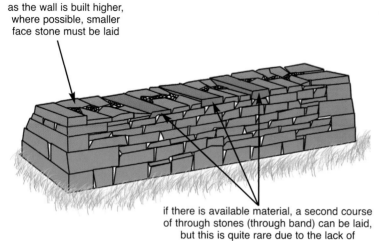

if there is available material, a second course
of through stones (through band) can be laid,
but this is quite rare due to the lack of
suitably sized stone on a walling site

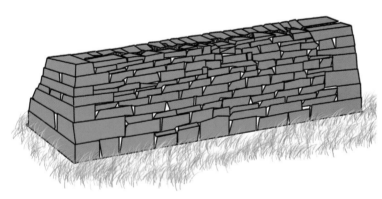

Wall built to a level just below the coping stones.

the end coping stones should be
the largest and heaviest available;
they act as 'book-ends'

Completed dry stione wall with coping stone.

Plan cross-section of the dry stone wall.

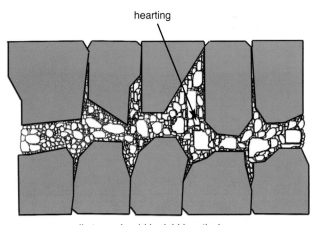

hearting

all stone should be laid lengthwise
into the wall where ever possible

correct

Foundation techniques.

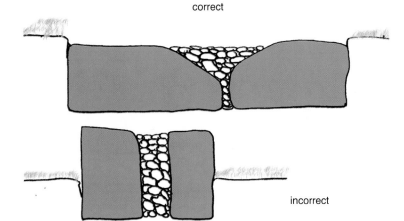

incorrect

face stone pinned
from behind

face stone
(front of
the wall)

face stone
(front of
the wall)

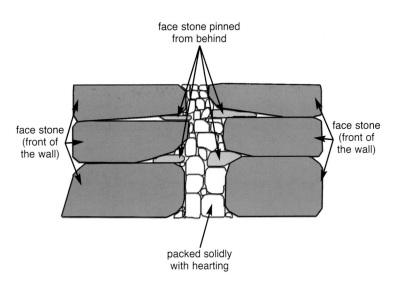

packed solidly
with hearting

Walling technique – correct.

117

the hearting is not inserted tightly enough
and the wall will collapse

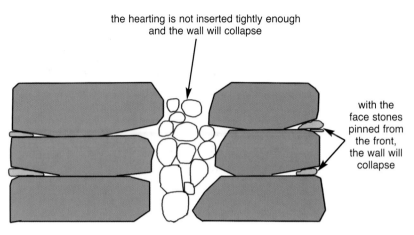

with the
face stones
pinned from
the front,
the wall will
collapse

the hearting and pinning are correct, but the positions of
the face stones will create an unstable dry stone wall

with the face
stones laid on
edge, the wall
will be
unstable and
could collapse
when settling

with the face
stones laid on
edge, the wall
will be
unstable and
could collapse
when settling

*Walling technique –
incorrect.*

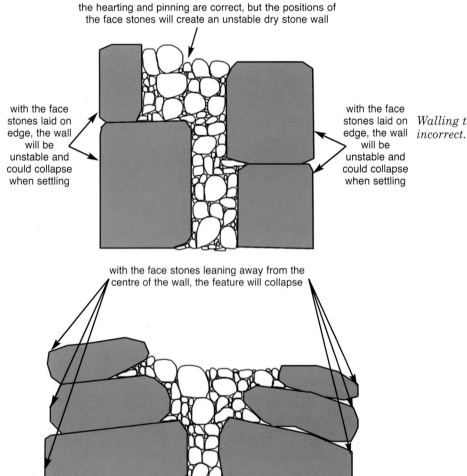

with the face stones leaning away from the
centre of the wall, the feature will collapse

*Walling technique –
incorrect.*

Sandstone will trim to size very easily, but cutting weathered limestone or slate can prove fairly difficult due to the brittle nature of the rock. Instead of breaking where expected, it will break from fissures, or split from the bedding plane. This can be annoying, but can be reduced by ensuring the face-stone is placed on a level surface, free from hard foreign bodies.

After finishing the two skins, fill the centre carefully with hearting. Do not throw or pour this material directly into the wall; instead, carefully place it by hand to protect the pinners under the face-stones. As a last job for this course, check the line of face-stones by looking down the entire length from one of the wall ends. If any stone appears misaligned, adjust in accordance with the string line. Using the methods just described, continue building the wall until half of its finished height is constructed. After this, the next important course is the 'through-band'.

The Through-Band

By the time the wall reaches the halfway mark, when all the lower courses are laid, at least half a ton of material per metre will be forcing its way toward the foundation stones. Up to the halfway point, the two skins of the wall will be able support themselves without too much difficulty. When the wall reaches its full height, however, the weight burden will double, resulting in a larger, uneven load on both sides of the wall. This burden will cause the wall to settle unevenly or, worse still, shift the lower face-stones so the wall begins to lean.

The idea behind the through-band is to bind the two skins on the lower courses together before extra weight is applied to the wall. The weight produced by the higher face-stones, once it is absorbed by the through-band, will distribute more evenly, dispersing the weight down the batter and through the courses. Before laying the through-band, build the higher course of face-stones as level as possible, and then raise the string lines out of the way to enable clear access to the wall. As with the foundation stones, throughs may require two people to carefully lift and lay them onto the course. The strain of lifting a heavy through could mean that it is dropped onto the wall. This, of course, will break or unsettle the face-stones below.

Through stones should be laid every 2–3ft (60–90cm) along the course, with their flattest and widest areas resting on the stones below. Usually, pinning should not be required, but any gaps underneath must be packed with hearting. If the stone is longer than the width of the course, move it so that the point of balance is resting on the centre, even if it means that both ends protrude out of the wall. Through stones are difficult to cut at the best of times, more so if the material is brittle in nature. It is far better to break the aesthetics of a smooth face than it is to break an important through down the wrong fissure, for this size of stone, in any large quantity, is usually uncommon. Use this philosophy for the end-stones once the wall's batter becomes narrow.

Constructing the Higher Courses

If the string lines have been moved to accommodate the through-band, reset them to just above the highest stones on the course. Concentrate on building the gaps between each through-stone, bringing the wall as level as possible. To further reinforce the weight-bearing nature of the through-band, lay face-stones that are able to run into the centre of the wall and rest on the hearting. Try to achieve this on both sides throughout the entire course, but if the supply of adequate material is limited, place these larger stones at equal intervals along the course, laying smaller face-stone in between.

Constructing the higher sections of wall follows the same methods described for the lower half, with a couple of exceptions. Firstly, you will find that the walling surface is narrower and will, by default, require smaller face-stones to accommodate the building of two skins. This may result in the need for more hammer work to trim stone to size. Secondly, as the wall begins to reach full height the quantity of walling material obviously diminishes. The latter could become frustrating when looking for an ideal face-stone and an uncertainty of the amount of material left to finish the job may creep in also. If the quantities of random walling have been worked out correctly, 1 ton of stone per metre of a wall built to the height of 4ft 6in (1.4m), there should be no problem. On rare occasions, where stone has been broken, or used elsewhere in the garden, then the task may require an extra, small load of walling stone.

Start building on the through-band after raising the string lines no more than 5in (13cm) above the course. Lay the end-stones first, then create a level course by laying the face-stones in between, using the same method as already discussed for the lower half of the wall. The last few courses of stone should consist of smaller material. If there is any large material left over at this stage, it can be broken up with a sledgehammer in order to produce the smaller size needed.

The penultimate course is the most critical and possibly the most unstable of all dry stone walling features. This is because it contains very small stone that will have to sustain the initial weight of the coping stones, and this material is very difficult to pin. All of the face-stones on the higher courses, without exception, must be laid with their lengths running into the centre of the wall, with each one tightly abutted against its neighbour. Stone that is placed with its longest face to the front will pivot out when the wall begins to settle; this will disturb the coping and result in the premature decay of the upper courses.

The Coping Stones
The course of coping acts as the wall's first shield of defence against the natural elements and the damage that can be caused by animals and people. The coping seals the top of the wall by bridging the two skins, thus binding both skins together. A wall that is missing coping will quickly deteriorate course by course. The top of any dry stone structure, without exception, should not be left unprotected.

Types of coping can vary and are not governed by any regional style. It is good practice, however, to copy the characteristics of the walls in your locality. Vertical stones, locked tightly together to form a continuous row, are the most commonly seen design of top stones.

As with the lower courses, start the coping by laying the end stones first. These should be heavy, large and entirely self-supporting, so they can rest on the wall without having to be pinned. Two strong coping stones at either end of the course will act like bookends for the ones that are laid in between and will stop the coping layer from falling off the end.

Once the two end-stones are on, a string line can be used as guide for the height of the finished course. Tie the line to a pin (you could make use of six-inch nail here) and insert it into a crevice in one of the wall ends. Stretch the string over the top of the end coping stone and pull it tightly over the one at the opposite end. Again, anchor the line in the wall-end. On longer stretches of wall, a third coping stone can be placed halfway down the course to prevent the string line from sagging.

Work from one end and place each coping stone firmly against its neighbour, making sure that it is as tight a fit as possible. More importantly, its full weight should rest on the two skins of face-stones. If the coping stone requires pinning, it should be inserted from the side facing down the course and pushed completely underneath to allow room for the next coping stone to abut against it. If the coping is of varied height, which is the case in most situations, sections of the penultimate course should be built up or taken away and then re-pinned and refilled with hearting.

CHAPTER ELEVEN

Some Ideas for Plants

Choosing plants and flowers is up to personal taste and I can only give some recommendations based on scent, all-year colour and wildlife attraction.

BUDDLEIA (Butterfly Bush)
A startling, summer flowering bush. Easy to grow and comes in many varieties. *B. davidii* – Royal Red and Empire Blue. Maximum height 9ft, maximum width 9ft

CARYOPTERIS (Blue Spiraea)
A rounded shrub, excellent for the fronts of borders. Maximum height 3ft (0.9m), maximum width 3ft. Clusters of fluffy, blue, fragrant flowers in August and September.

CEANOTHUS (Californian Lilac)
A very attractive blue shrub flowering in late summer and autumn. Maximum height 4ft (1.2m), maximum width 4ft.

CERATOSTIGMA (Hardy Plumbago)
A low-growing shrub. Blossoms in summer with cluster of bright blue, phlox-like flowers. Maximum height 2ft (0.6m) but may reach 3ft (0.9m) when planted in a sheltered place.

CHOISYA (Mexican Orange Blossom)
A neat, rounded, evergreen bush. Its white, starry flowers appear in May and occasionally throughout the summer. Maximum height 6ft (1.8m).

CISTUS (Rock Rose)
A small and attractive bush, flowering in June and July. Its delicate petals open in the morning and fall by nightfall. Nevertheless, new buds appear regularly throughout the flowering season.

CORNUS (Dogwood)
Dogwood is particularly useful for the all-year colour garden. Their attractive stems help to colour the winter garden and produce berries for wildlife. Maximum height 8ft (2.4m).

CORYLOPSIS (Winter Hazel)
Similar to its relative the witch hazel, this shrub produces yellow flowers before the leaves appear. The fragrant blooms appear March/April. Usual height is 6ft (1.8m).

COTONEASTER
Dwarf evergreen shrub producing red, winter berries for wildlife. During May this shrub produces pea-like flowers. Depending on the variegation available, the flowers can be yellow, pink or white. The dwarf variety is ideal for ground cover.

ELAEAGNUS (Oleaster)
With its yellow and green leaves the oleaster will brighten up the winter border. This shrub produces small, fragrant flowers, but the plant is mainly grown for its foliage and winter berries. Maximum height 8ft (2.4m).

ESCALLONIA

Escallonia grows an abundance of shiny leaves and tubular flowers. This evergreen plant is ideal for borders, bearing clusters of white, pink and red flowers from June to early autumn. Average height 6ft (1.8m).

FORSYTHIA (Golden Bells)

Forsythia is grown mainly for its abundance of yellow flowers during March and April. It can either be grown against a wall or as part of an ornamental border. Maximum height 4ft (1.2m).

GARRYA (Silk Tassel Bush)

The striking feature of *Garrya* is its long, silken catkins during January and February. This is an ideal shrub for the all-year garden because of its evergreen, glossy foliage. Maximum height 9ft (2.7m).

HEBE (Veronica)

Small, fragrant evergreen shrub with shiny, oval leaves and spikes of small, blue or white flowers. Blossoms throughout the summer and into autumn. A small shrub, ideal for the front of borders.

HYPERICUM (St John's Wort)

A low growing shrub, spreading rapidly to suppress weed growth. Yellow flowers from June to September. Maximum height 3ft (0.9m).

KALMIA

Sometimes called the mountain laurel or calico bush (*K. latifolia*). This shrub grows wild in North America. The flower clusters resemble Chinese lanterns; they then open into saucer-shaped flowers of delicate pink.

KERRIA (Jew's Mellow)

With its attractive, serrated leaves, *Kerria* produces an abundance of yellow flowers in April and May. Maximum height 6ft (1.8m).

KOLKWITZIA (Beauty Bush)

An easy-to-grow shrub, thriving in all types of soil. During May and June its weeping stems are festooned with pink, bell-shaped flowers. Low growing with a good spread, ideal for suppressing weed growth.

LAVANDULA (Lavender)

An all-time favourite in British gardens. This shrub produces aromatic flowers and foliage. Blue flowers appear in July to September. Maximum height 3ft (0.9m).

MAHONIA

An evergreen shrub, resembling holly. This shrub produces fragrant, yellow flowers early in the year.

MYRTUS (Myrtle)

A sweet smelling bush with the fragrance arising from its white flowers and leaves. Maximum height 3ft (0.9m).

OSMANTHUS

This evergreen shrub is neat and well rounded. Its white flowers produce a jasmine-like fragrance. Maximum height 6ft (1.8m).

PEROVSKIA (Russian Sage)

A fragrant bush with blue flowers. Ideal plant for the herbaceous border. Maximum height 4ft (1.2m).

PHILADELPHUS (Mock Orange)

Philadelphus's white flowers appear in June and July. Its orange-blossom fragrance can be detected some distance away on warm, summer evenings. Maximum height 6ft (1.8m).

PIERIS (Andromeda)

An evergreen shrub with dense foliage. Flowers in April or May.

POTENTILLA (Shrubby Cinquefoil)

Flowers from May through to September. Orange or white blooms. Maximum height 3ft (0.9m).

RHODODENDRON

Evergreen shrub which originated in the Himalayas and was transported to Britain for game cover. The new dwarf varieties are not as pernicious as their spreading relatives. An evergreen shrub, producing striking blooms as early as February and as late as August. Maximum height 4ft (1.2m) (dwarf).

AZALEA

Similar to the rhododendron, the azalea produces clusters of flowers during May. Maximum height 4ft (1.2m) (dwarf).

BETULA PENDULA (Weeping Birch)

A beautiful weeping tree with silver bark. Ideal for small gardens as its root system is shallow and does not impact built structures if planted in the right position.

Useful Contacts

CONTACTS FOR NATURAL STONE

Architectural Stone Quarry Supplies
UK-wide internet-based stone quarry merchant that deals in York Stone, paving stone, landscaping stone, rockery stone, patio stone, garden stone and stone kerbs and stone copings to the public and to other stone merchants in the stone merchant industry.
www.architecturalstonesupplies.co.uk

Aggregate Industries UK
A major producer and supplier of primary, secondary and recycled construction aggregates, asphalt, ready-mixed concrete and pre-cast concrete products. UK coverage.
www.aggregate-uk.com

Albion Stone Quarries Ltd
Supplies dimension stone blocks, slabs, tiles and masonry in Portland Stone and other limestones.
www.albionstonequarries.com

Bath Stone Group
Stoke Ground Bath Stone is used throughout the UK in both restoration and new build projects.
www.bath-stone.co.uk

Berwyn Slate Quarry Ltd
North-east Wales. Berwyn Slate Quarry produces a rich blue-black natural Welsh slate suitable for many building and architectural purposes.
www.berwynslate.com

Dennis Gillson and Son
Producers of York Stone.
www.gillsons.com

Dunhouse Natural Stone
County Durham. 'Dunhouse Quarries have seventy-five years' experience in the quarrying and supply of dimensional building stone. We pride ourselves on being one of the UK's leading suppliers and offer a portfolio of natural stones for the construction industry.'
www.dunhouse.co.uk

Greaves Welsh Slate Company Ltd
Llechwedd slate quarry near Blaenau Ffestiniog in North Wales.
www.llechwedd.co.uk

Hillhouse Quarry Group
South-western Scotland. Manufacturers of dry coated stone and concrete products.
www.hillhousegroup.co.uk

Kirkstone Quarries Ltd

Cumbria. Produces a wide variety of stone products.
www.kirkstone.com

Leith's (Scotland) Ltd

Quarries in the north of Scotland and produces a wide range of products.
www.leiths-group.co.uk

Lloyd Spar Quarries North Wales

Aggregates and quarry products for the construction and landscaping industry.
www.lloyds-spar.co.uk

Midland Quarry Products

Suppliers of hard rock and asphalt (coated materials), providing a comprehensive range of aggregates and asphalt products to the construction, civil engineering and rail industries.
www.mqp.co.uk

Realstone

UK-wide suppliers of natural stone to the building industry. Also quarrying, cutting, masonry, carving stone for traditional restoration, new build and landscaping projects.
www.realstone.co.uk

Stanleys Quarry

Gloucestershire. Suppliers of building stone and internal flagstone.
www.cotswoldstone.com

Tennants Scottish Cobbles

Suppliers of Scottish cobbles from its quarry.
www.scottishcobbles.com

The following information was kindly supplied by Tony McCormack,
www.pavingexpert.com

Acorn Stone Merchants Ltd

Hard landscaping stone
Kirby Road
Lomeshaye Industrial Estate
Nelson
Lancashire   BB9 6RS
Tel: 01282 612211
Fax: 01282 619666

Alfred McAlpine Slate

Slate for paving and roofing
Penrhyn Quarry
Bethesda
Bangor
North Wales   LL57 4YG
Tel: 01248 600656
Fax: 01248 601171

Architectural Stone (UK) Ltd

New and reclaimed stone
Unit 3
Crow Lane
Ramsbottom
Lancashire   BL0 9BR
Tel: 01706 82171
Fax: 01706 210240

Architectural Stone Supplies

Reclaimed stone
Owl Hall Cottage
Plantation Road
Accrington
Lancashire   BB5 2DQ
Tel: 01254 397277

Bannold

Paving, rockery stone and decorative aggregates
Bannold Road
Waterbeach
Cambridge   CB5 9RB
Tel: 0500 012231
Fax: 01223 565431

Bardon Natural Stone
New setts and flags
Thorney Mill Road
West Drayton
Middlesex   UB7 7EZ
Tel: 01895 442852
Fax: 01895 421464

BBS Brick & Stone Ltd
Landscaping stone specialists
Trident House
106 Barnsley Road
Sandal, Wakefield
West Yorkshire   WF1 5NX
Tel: 01924 241100
Fax: 01924 250530

Bingley Stone Centre
New and reclaimed stone paving
Cullingworth Mills, Cullingworth
West Yorks   BD13 5AB
Tel: 01535 273813
Fax: 01535 273194

Bridge Street Stone
Imported stone paving
Bridge Street South
Colne
Lancashire   BB8 0DR
Tel: 01282 860571
Fax: 01282 867446

British Stone
Trade body promoting stone from British quarries
77 Compton Road
Wolverhampton
West Midlands   WV3 9QH
Tel: 01902 717789
Fax: 01902 717789

Burlington Slate Ltd
Distinctively green lakeland stone and slate
Cavendish House
Kirkby-in-Furness
Cumbria   LA17 7UN
Tel: 01229 889 661
Fax: 01229 889 466

A & D Sutherland Ltd
Caithness flagstone for paving
Spittal Quarry
By Watten
Caithness   KW1 5XR
Tel: 01847 841239
Fax: 01847 841321

Caithness Stone Industries
Caithness stone for paving and decorative uses
The Shore
Wick
Caithness   KW1 4JW
Tel: 01955 605472
Fax: 01955 605907

CED Ltd
Stone paving and landscape supplies
728 London Road
West Thurrock
Grays, Essex   RM20 3LU
Tel: 01708 867237
Fax: 01708 867230

Charcon
Natural stone setts, kerbs and paving in granite, York stone and sandstone
Hulland Ward
Ashbourne
Derbyshire   DE6 3ET
Tel: 01335 372222
Fax: 01335 3700

Cloburn Quarry
Granite aggregates and pavings
Pettinain
Lanark   ML11 8SR
Tel: 01555 663444
Fax: 01555 664111

The Completely Stoned Company Ltd
Reclaimed stone paving
Wedhampton Manor
Devizes
Wiltshire   SN10 3QE
Tel: 01380 840092
Fax: 01380 840093

Delabole Slate
Cornish stone for paving, roofing and building
Pengelly Road
Delabole
Cornwall
PL33 9AZ
Tel: 01840 212242
Fax: 01840 212948

Dimensional Stone Ltd
Building stone
Crossgate Road
Park Farm Industrial Estate
Redditch
Worcestershire
B98 7SN
Tel: 01527 510515
Fax: 01527 510585

Dunhouse Quarry Ltd
Traditional stone for masonry and paving
Dunhouse Quarry Works
Staindrop
Darlington
County Durham
DL2 3QU
Tel: 01833 660208
Fax: 01833 660749

Ennstone Johnston plc
Aggregates, including the famous 'Breedon Gravel'
Breedon Quarry
Breedon on the Hill
Derby
DE73 1PA
Tel: 01332 862254
Fax: 01332 863149

Fyfe Glenrock
Granite for paving and architecture
Enterprise Drive
Westhill
Aberdeenshire   AB32 6TQ
Tel: 01224 744101
Tel: 01224 743911

George Farrar (Quarries) Ltd
Paving and building stone
Bradford Street
Keighley
West Yorkshire
BD21 3EB
Tel: 01535 602344
Fax: 01535 606247

Gallop & Rivers
Architectural antiques, reclaimed and imported paving Ty-rash
Brecon Road
Crickhowell
Powys
NP8 1SF
Tel: 01873 811084
Fax: 01873 811084

Global Stone (Colchester) Ltd
Imported stone paving flags, cubes and setts
129–139, Layer Road
Colchester
Essex
CO2 9JY
Tel: 01206 766032
Fax: 01206 543043

Hardrock Ltd
Paving and landscaping stone
Stoney Brow Quarry
Upholland
Skelemersdale
Lancashire
WN8 0QE
Tel: 0800 542 8679
Tel: 01695 622950

Hardscape
Materials for commercial hardscapes
14 Ashworth House
Deakins Business Park
Egerton
Bolton
Lancashire   BL7 9RP
Tel: 01204 590666
Fax: 01204 590620

Harris Slate and Stone
Slate and stone importers and distributors
Units 2, 4 & 5
Firsdale Ind Est
Nangreaves Street
Leigh
Lancashire
WN7 4TN
Tel: 01942 607800
Fax: 01942 671779

Indi Stone
*Importer and distributor of natural stone
products*
1 Rycroft Avenue
Deeping St James
Peterborough
Cambridgeshire
PE6 8NT
Tel: 01778 342567
Fax: 01778 342778

Inigo Jones & Co. Ltd
Crafted Welsh slate
Y Groeslon
Caernarfon
Gwynedd
LL54 7ST
Tel: 01286 830242
Fax: 01286 831247

Irish Aggregates (Munster) Ltd
*Stone for paving and building and a wide
selection of aggregates*
Classis
Ovens
Co. Cork
Ireland
Tel: +353 (0) 21 487 2733
Fax: +353 (0) 21 487 1705

Johnsons Wellfield Quarries Ltd
Genuine hard York stone
Crosland Hill
Huddersfield
West Yorkshire   HD4 7AB
Tel: 01484 652311
Fax: 01484 460007

J. Suttle Swanage Quarries
Quarried aggregates
Panorama Road
Swanage
Dorset
BH19 2QS
Tel: 01929 423576
Fax: 01929 427656

JW Stone & Brick Ltd
Natural stone paving
Unit G
Dafen Industrial Park
Llanelli
[county?]
SA14 8NS
Tel: 01554 770818

Kent Blaxill Ltd
Paving and landscaping materials
129-139 Layer Road
Colchester
Essex
CO2 9JY
Tel: 01206 216000
Fax: 01206 762981

Kirk Natural Stone
Imported and local stone for paving
Bridgend
Fyvie
Turriff
Aberdeenshire
AB53 8QB
Tel: 01651 891891
Fax: 01651 891891

Kirkstone Ltd
Architectural stone
Skelwith Bridge
Ambleside
Cumbria
LA22 9NN
Tel: 015394 33296
Fax: 015394 34006

Knockdown Stone
*Traditionally cut Cotswold stone for roofing,
building and gardening projects*
Halfway Bush Farm
Tetbury
Gloucestershire
GL8 8QY
Tel: 01666 840443

Ladycross Quarry
*Hand-quarried Northumberland slate for
paving and walling*
Ladycross Quarry
Slaley
Hexham
Northumberland
NE47 0BY
Tel: 01434 673302
Fax: 01434 601151

Landscaping Supplies Ltd
Imported stone and decorative aggregates
c/o AE Roberts Ltd
Gravel Hill
Shirrel Heath
Southampton
Hampshire   SO32 2JQ
Tel: 01329 510962
Fax: 01329 505281

Lunts Heath Building Supplies
*Retailer of natural stone, concrete paving
flags and blocks, decorative aggregates, tools
and general building supplies*
Heath Road
Widnes
Cheshire   WA8 5RZ
Tel: 0151 424 4571
Fax: 0151 424 5200

Marshalls Ltd
*Paving and building stone, quarried
aggregates*
Southowram
Halifax
West Yorkshire   HX3 9SY
Tel: 01422 306000
Fax: 01422 330185

McMonagle Stone
Donegal quartzite and sandstone
Mountcharles
Co. Donegal
Ireland
Tel: +353 (0) 74 973 5061
Fax: +353 (0) 74 973 5408

Midlands Slate & Tile
Reclaimed and imported stone for paving
Qualcast Road, Horseley Fields
Wolverhampton
West Midlands
Tel: 01902 790473
Fax: 01902 791354

Moher Flagstone
Distinctive Liscannor slate for paving
Cois na Mara
Ballycotton
Co. Cork
Ireland
Tel: 00353 (0)214 645971

Natural Paving Products (UK) Ltd
*Manufacturer, importer and distributor of
natural stone landscaping products*
Sandtoft Grange Airfield
Sandtoft
Thorne
Doncaster
South Yorkshire
DN8 5SU
Tel: 0870 242 3018
Fax: 0870 242 2118

The Natural Slate Company
Imported slate for paving and tiling
Unit 2
Armytage Estate
Station Road
Whittington Moor
Chesterfield
Derbyshire
S41 9ET
Tel: 01246 452495

The Original Stone Paving Company
Specialist stone paving contractors
Wrexham
Clywd
Tel: 01978 661000
Fax: 01978 661000

Peyton's Pavings
Imported stone flags
121 High Street
Harston
Cambridge
CB2 5QB
Tel: 01223 870711
Fax: 01223 874445

Pickard Group Ltd
Natural hard York stone from
Bolton Wood Quarry
Fagley Quarry, Fagley Lane
Eccleshill
Bradford
West Yorkshire
BD2 3NT
Tel: 01274 637307
Fax: 01274 626146

Pinks Hill Landscape Merchants Ltd
Paving stone and gravels
Bourne Mill Industrial Estate
Guildford Road
Farnham
Surrey
GU9 9PS
Tel: 01252 727 900
Fax: 01252 727 999

Pomery Natural Stone Ltd
Stone for paving and landscaping
37 Glenavon Gardens
Slough
Berkshire
SL3 7HW
Tel: 01753 533505
Fax: 01753 533961

Purpletree Ltd
British and imported paving stone
Home Farm Offices
Hartforth
Richmond
North Yorkshire
DL10 5JS
Tel: 01748 850896
Fax: 01748 821952

Ransford's
Stone paving and flooring
Drayton Way, Drayton Fields
Daventry
Northamptonshire
NN11 5XW
Tel: 01327 705310
Fax: 01327 706831

The Rare Stone Group
Architectural stone
184 Nottingham Road
Mansfield
Nottinghamshire
NG18 5AP
Tel: 01623 623092
Fax: 01623 622509

Realstone Ltd
Newly quarried British stone
Wingerworth
Chesterfield
Derbyshire
S42 6RG
Tel: 01246 270244
Fax: 01246 220095

Ribble Reclamation
Architectural salvage
Ducie Place
Off New Hall Lane
Preston
Lancashire
Tel: 01772 794534
Fax: 01772 794604

Rivendale Stone
Imported paving stone
629–637 Upper Newtownards Road
Belfast
BT4 3LR
Tel: 028 9048 5227
Fax: 028 9048 7694

Riverside Reclamation
Reclaimed stone paving
Raikes Clough Industrial Estate
Raikes Lane
Bolton
Lancashire
BL3 1RP
Tel: 01204 533141
Fax: 01204 534401

Rock Unique Ltd
Stone for landscaping
Main Road
Sundridge
Sevenoaks
Kent
TN14 6ED
Tel: 01959 565608
Fax: 01959 569312

Romsey Reclamation
Reclaimed stone and other salvaged materials
Station Approach
Romsey Train Station
Romsey
Hampshire
SO51 8DU
Tel: 01794 524174
Fax: 01794 514344

Russell Stone Merchants
New and reclaimed York stone, gritstone and sandstone for paving and masonry
Westside Mills
Ripley Road
Bradford
West Yorkshire
BD4 7EX
Tel: 01274 727200
Fax: 01274 392127

Ryanstone
Granite paving and statuary
Blessington
Co. Wicklow
Ireland
Tel: +353 45 865139
Fax: +353 45 865747
In UK: 01418 848266

S & N Granite
Granite setts and flagstones
The Bay, Camolin
Enniscorthy
Co. Wexford
Ireland
Tel: +353 54 83992
Fax: +353 54 83992

St Albans Stone
Imported flagstones
2 Bridge Cottage
Sandridgebury Lane
St Albans
Hertfordshire
Tel: 01727 831211
Fax: 01727 831211

Sharman Brothers
New and reclaimed York flagstones
Slack End Stone Yard
Swales Moor Road
Halifax
West Yorkshire
HX3 6UF
Tel: 01274 816384

Simply Stoned
Reclaimed Scottish granite and whinstone
56 Smithstone Crescent
Croy
Falkirk
G65 9HG
Tel: 01236 822607

Stancliffe Stone Co Ltd
British stone for paving and masonry
Grangemill
Matlock
Derbyshire
DE4 4BW
Tel: 01629 650859
Fax: 01629 650996

Steptoe's Yard
Reclaimed stone paving
Park Close Quarry
Moor Lane
Salterforth
Barnoldswick
Lancashire
BB18 5SP
Tel: 01282 813313
Fax: 01282 841177

Stone Developments
*Irish natural stone, blue limestone for paving
and masonry*
4 The Metro Centre
Toutley Road
Wokingham
Berkshire
Tel: 0118 977 6926
Fax: 0118 977 6927

Stone Essentials
Building and landscaping stone
Unit 4 Mount Spring Works
Off Burnley Road East
Waterfoot
Rossendale
Lancashire
BB4 9LA
Tel: 01706 211120
Fax: 01706 228707

Stone Federation of Great Britain
Trade Association for the UK stone industry
Tel: 020 7608 5094

Stone Flair
Patio paving and natural stone
Lower Teme Business Park
Burford
Worcestershire
WR15 8HP
Tel: 0870 600 9111
Fax: 0870 600 9112

Stone-Mart
*Online information source for the UK stone
industry, www.stone-mart.co.uk*
104 St James Road
Prescot
Merseyside
L34 2SJ
Tel: 0151 289 0632
Fax: 0151 289 0632

Stonepave UK Ltd
Stone for hard landscaping
Unit 2
The Terrace
Lutterworth
Leicestershire
LE17 4BW
Tel: 01455 559777
Fax: 01455 559111

The Stone Paving Company
Reclaimed stone paving
Redhall Lane
Penley
Wrexham
Clwyd
Tel: 01978 710233
Fax: 0194 874460

Stonescape
Reclaimed and new stone setts, cubes and flag paving
The Stone Centre
Ince Moss Industrial Estate
Cemetery Road
Ince
Wigan
Lancashire
WN3 4NN
Tel: 01942 866666
Fax: 01942 866661

The Stonewood Co.
New and reclaimed stone and timber products, specialist stone matching service
101 Nora Street
Barrowford
Nelson
Lancashire
BB9 8NT
Tel: 01282 612297

Stone World
Paving, walling and aggregates
Stoneworld (Oxon) Ltd
Views Farm
Windmill Hill
Great Milton
Oxfordshire
OX44 7NW
Tel: 01844 279274
Fax: 01844 278643

Tobermore Concrete Products Ltd
Sandstone and granite for paving
Dungiven Road
Tobermore
Londonderry
BT45 5QF
Tel: 028 796 42411
Fax: 028 796 44145

Trent Stone and Walling Ltd
New and reclaimed stone specialists
87 Bingham Road
Radcliffe on Trent
Nottinghamshire
NG12 2GP
Tel: 0115 933 4499
Fax: 0115 933 2139

Westminster Stone Company Ltd
Imported and York stone flags, setts, cobbles and decorative aggregates
Shaws Estate
Sodylt
Ellesmere
Shropshire
SY12 9EL
Tel: 01978 710685
Fax: 01978 710844

Whitehall Stone Sales Ltd
New and reclaimed York stone for paving
Quarrie Works Yard
Law Street
Bradford
West Yorkshire
BD4 9NF
Tel: 01274 684440
Fax: 01274 684108

Woodkirk Stone Ltd
Newly quarried paving, walling and roofing stone
Britannia Quarries
Rein Road
Morley
Leeds
West Yorkshire
LS27 0SW
Tel: 0113 253 0464
Fax: 0113 252 7520

OTHER USEFUL CONTACTS

The Dry Stone Walling Association of Great Britain (DSWA)
Registered Charity 289678
PO Box 8615
Sutton Coldfield
B75 7HQ
Tel/fax: 0121 378 0493
E-mail: j.simkins@dswa.org.uk
Website: www.dswa.org.uk

Serving the craft of dry stone walling throughout Britain, and beyond. The Dry Stone Walling Association of Great Britain, founded in 1968, is a democratic, members' organization and registered charity. There are branches in most upland areas of Britain. DSWA currently has 1,200 members of whom 250 are professional wallers and dykers.

The Association works to promote all aspects of the craft of dry stone walling. This includes publication of an annual Register of Certificated Professional Wallers, a series of technical specifications, plus a leaflet detailing courses. DSWA operates the only tiered crafts skills certification scheme in Britain and which involves work being carried out in presence of examiners: the Craftsman Certification Scheme.

British Trust for Conservation Volunteers (BTCV)
Registered Charity 261009
36 St Mary's Street
Wallingford
OX10 0EU
Telephone: 01491 821600

The BTCV is Britain's largest volunteer conservation body. They offer training courses on every aspect of practical conservation and work alongside local authorities, National Parks and industry, among others, on practical conservation projects. This highly professional and well-organized body offers a range of conservation holidays both at home and abroad. The range of skills that can be attained through the BTCV is boundless.

Peak Park Planning Board
Aldern House
Bakewell
Derbyshire
Contact: Pete Hardwick (Volunteers Organizer)

The Peak District National Park offers many volunteering opportunities. They continually run a host of conservation projects during the week and at weekends, and the chance to learn new skills or enhance existing ones is immense. Brunts Barn, their purpose-built volunteers centre, is second to none and their highly trained full-time and part-time staff are always eager to disseminate what they know.

USEFUL WEBSITES

ADAS: www.adas.co.uk/index.htm

British Trust for Conservation Volunteers (BTCV): www.btcv.org

Common Ground: www.commonground.org.uk

Council for the Protection of Rural England (CPRE): www.greenchannel.com/cpre

Council for the Protection of Rural Wales (CPRW): www.cprw.org.uk/Default.htm

Council for National Parks (CNP): www.councilfornationalparks.freeserve.co.uk

The Countryside Agency (CA): www.countryside.gov.uk

Countryside Council for Wales (CCW): www.ccw.gov.uk

Department of Agriculture and Rural development for Northern Ireland: www.dani.gov.uk

English Heritage: www.english-heritage.org.uk

English Nature (EN): www.english-nature.org.uk

Farming and Wildlife Advisory Group (FWAG): www.snw.org.uk/enwweb/fwag.htm

Historic Scotland: www.historic-scotland.gov.uk

Ministry of Agriculture, Fisheries and Food (MAFF): www.maff.gov.uk/maffhome.htm

National Assembly for Wales: www.wales.gov.uk

Ramblers Association (RA): www.ramblers.org.uk

RIGS (Regionally Important Geological & Geomorphological Sites): www.ukrigs.org.uk

Royal Town Planning Institute (RTPI): www.rtpi.co.uk/advice/index.htm

Scottish Natural Heritage (SNH): www.snh.org.uk

Scottish Office: www.scotland.gov.uk/whatwedo.asp

Shell: www.shell.co.uk/flash/index.html.

Welsh Historic Monuments: www.castlewales.com/cadw.html

Women's Institute (WI): www.nfwi.org.uk

Glossary

A-frame, batter frame – A wooden device used as a guide for building a wall to the correct angle or batter.

Agate – A variegated variety of quartz showing coloured bands or other markings (clouded, moss-like, etc).

Anchors – Anchors for stonework include those made of flat stock (strap, cramps, dovetails, dowel, strap and dowel, and two-way anchors) and round stock (rod cramp, rod anchor, eyebolt and dowel, flat-hood wall and dowel and wire toggle bolt).

Argillite – A compact sedimentary rock composed mainly of clay and aluminium silicate minerals.

Arkose – A sandstone containing 10 per cent or more clastic grains of feldspar. Also called arkosic sandstone, feldspathic sandstone.

Ashlar – Masonry having a face of square or rectangular stones, either smooth or textured.

Baluster – A dense textured (aphanitic), igneous rock relatively high in iron and magnesia minerals and relatively low in silica, generally dark grey to black and feldspathic; a general term in contradistinction to felsite. A light-coloured feldspathic and highly siliceous rock of similar texture and origin.

Batter – The angle on which a wall is constructed.

Black granite – Rock species known to petrologists as diabase, diorite, gabbro and intermediate varieties, are sometimes quarried as building stone, chiefly for ornamental use, and sold as 'black granite'. As dimension blocks or slabs, they are valued specifically for their dark grey to black colour when polished. Scientifically, they are far removed in composition from true granites, though they may be satisfactorily used for some of the purposes to which commercial granites are adapted. They possess an interlocking crystalline texture, but unlike granite, they contain little or no quartz or alkaline feldspar, and are characterized by an abundance of one or more of the common black rock-forming minerals (chiefly pyroxenes, hornblende and biotite).

Bluestone – A dense, hard, fine-grained, commonly feldspathic sandstone or siltstone of medium to dark or bluish-grey colour that splits readily along original bedding planes to form thin slabs. The stones of Stonehenge are bluestones.

Bolt hole – Small access point at the base of a wall for the purpose of catching rabbits.

Bond stone – Used in varying percentages to anchor or bond the stone veneer to the backing material. Bond stones are generally cut to twice the bed thickness of the material being used.

Border stone – Usually a flat stone used as an edging material. A border stone is generally used to retain the field of the terrace or platform.

Bridging joins – The process of crossing the joins of face-stones on a dry stone wall or mortared brick wall.

Broach – To drill or cut out material left between closely spaced drill holes; a mason's sharp-pointed chisel for dressing stone.

136

Brownstone – Sandstone of characteristic brown or reddish-brown colour, caused by a large amount of iron oxide as interstitial material.

Brushed finish – Obtained by brushing the stone with a coarse rotary-type wire brush.

Building stone, natural – Rock material in its natural state of composition and aggregation as it exists in the quarry and is usable in construction as dimension building stone.

Bull nose – Convex rounding of a stone member, such as a stair tread.

Calcarenite – Limestone composed predominantly of clastic sand-size grains of calcite.

Calcite streaks – Description of a white or milky-like streak occurring in stone. It is a joint plane usually wider than a glass seam and has been re-cemented by deposition of calcite in the crack and is structurally sound.

Capital – The culminating stone at the top of a column or pilaster, often richly carved.

Carve – Shaping a design to form by cutting – the trade of a sculptor.

Cleavage plane or bedding plane – Plane or planes along which a stone may likely break.

Cleavage – The ability of a rock mass to break along natural surfaces; a surface of natural parting.

Coating – A protective or decorative covering applied to the surface or impregnated into stone for such purposes as waterproofing, enhancing resistance to weathering, wear and chemical action, or improving the appearance of the stone.

Cobblestone – A natural rounded stone, large enough for use in paving; commonly used to describe paving blocks, usually granite, generally cut to rectangular shapes.

Commercial marble – A crystalline rock composed predominantly of calcite, dolomite and/or serpentine, and capable of taking a polish.

Coping – A flat stone used as a cap on free-standing walls.

Course – A horizontal range of stone units the length of the wall.

Crack – A break, split, fracture, fissure, separation, cleavage or elongated narrow opening within natural stone.

Crazy paving – A style of random stone hard-standing.

Cross fall – The slope of a patio that directs rainwater away from dwellings and enables water run-off, avoiding puddles on the surface.

Crowfoot (styoite) – Description of a dark grey to black zigzag marking occurring in stone. Usually structurally sound.

Crown – The top of a Devonshire hedge, Cornish hedge or Welsh Clawdd. Usually made of turf, which is formed into a dome.

Crystalline limestone – A limestone, either calcitic or dolomitic, composed of interlocking crystalline grains of the constituent minerals and of phaneritic texture.

Curbing – Slabs and blocks of stone bordering streets or footpaths.

Cut stone – Stone fabricated to specific dimensions.

Cutting stock – A term used to describe slabs of varying size, finish and thickness, which are used in fabricating tread, risers, copings, borders, sills, stools, hearths, mantels, and other special-purpose stones.

Dacite – A fine-grained, extrusive (volcanic) rock, intermediate in colour and composition between basalt and rhyolite.

Dimension stone – Natural building stone that has been selected, trimmed or cut to specified or indicated shapes or sizes with or without one or more mechanically dressed surfaces.

Dolomitic limestone – A limestone rich in magnesium carbonate, frequently somewhat crystalline in character, found in ledge formations in a wide variety of colour tones and textures. Generally speaking, its crushing and tensile strengths are greater than oolitic limestone and its appearance shows greater variety in texture.

Dowel – A short piece of non-ferrous metal or slate fixed into a mortise or sinking in the joints of adjoining stones to prevent movement.

Dressed or hand-dressed – The cutting of rough chunks of stone by hand to create a square or rectangular shape. A stone that is sold as dressed stone generally refers to stone ready for installation. Sometimes called scabbling.

Dressed stone – Stone cut on all sides to form attractive faces.

Dressing stone – The act of cutting natural stone to any desired shape.

Drip – A recess cut under a sill or projecting stone to throw off water, preventing it from running down the face of the wall or other surface, such as a window or door.

Dripstone – A projecting moulding over the heads of doorways, windows and archways to throw off the rain. Also known as a 'hood-mould' and, when rectangular, as a 'label'.

Dry stone wall – A stone wall that is constructed one stone upon the other without the use of any mortar.

Dry – An open or unhealed joint plane not filled with calcite and not structurally sound.

Durability – The measure of the ability of natural building stone to endure and to maintain its essential and distinctive characteristics of strength, resistance to decay, and appearance, with relation to a specific manner, purpose and environment of use.

Efflorescence – A crystalline deposit appearing on stone surfaces typically caused by soluble salts carried through or onto the stone by moisture, which has sometimes been found to come from brick, tile, concrete blocks, cement, mortar, concrete and similar materials in the wall or above.

End stones – Large stone used for constructing a wall end.

Entasis – The curve of the upper two-thirds of a column.

Exposed aggregate – Larger pieces of stone aggregate purposefully exposed for their colour and texture in a cast slab.

Face – The exposed portion of stone that faces out from a wall.

Ferruginous – Limestone or sandstone containing a high proportion of iron oxide.

Field stone – Loose blocks separated from ledges by natural processes and scattered through or upon the regolith ('soil') cover, applied also to similar transported materials, such as glacial boulders and cobbles.

Fines – The powder, dust, silt-size and sand-size material resulting from processing (usually crushing) rock.

Finish – Final surface applied to the face of stone during dressing.

Finished stone – Building stone with one or more dressed surfaces.

Flagstone – Thin slabs of stone used for flagging or paving walks, driveways, patios, etc. It is generally fine-grained sandstone, bluestone, quartzite or slate, but thin slabs of other stones may be used.

Fleuri cut – Cutting quarried marble or stone parallel to the natural bedding plane.

Foundation stones, foundation, footing, footings – The base of the wall.

Fracture – A break in rock produced by mechanical failure. Fractures include faults and joints.

Freestone – A stone that may be cut freely in any direction without fracture or splitting.

Gapping – The act of repairing a damaged section of wall.

Glass seam – Descriptions of a narrow glass-like streak occurring in stone; a joint plane that has been re-cemented by deposition of translucent calcite in the crack and structurally sound.

Grain – The easiest cleavage direction in a stone. Also, particles (crystals, sand grains, etc.) of rock.

Granite – A fine- to coarse-grained, igneous rock formed by volcanic action consisting of quartz, feldspar and mica, with accessory minerals. Granite-type rocks included those of similar texture and origin.

Granular – Having a texture characterized by particles that are apparent to the unaided eye. For sedimentary rocks, particles less than 4in (10mm) in diameter.

Gravel surface – A walking surface made up of fine stone.

Greenstone – Includes stones that have been metamorphosed or otherwise changed so that they have assumed a distinctive greenish colour owing to the presence of one or more of the following minerals: chlorite, epidote or actinolite.

Grout – Mortar of pouring consistency.

Hand-cut random rectangular ashlar – A pattern where all the stone is hand cut into squares and rectangulars. Joints are fairly consistent, similar to sawed-bed ashlar in appearance.

Hearting, harting, infill, rubble, centre stones – Small stone used to fill the gaps in middle of the wall.

Igneous – One of the three great classes of rock (igneous, sedimentary and metamorphic), solidified from molten state, such as granite and lavas.

Incise – To cut inwardly or engrave, as with an inscription.

Inscription – Lettering cut in stone.

Intermediate stones, face-stones – Stones used to build the section of wall between the coping and foundation.

Join – The space between stone units, usually filled with mortar.

Jumper – In ashlar patterns, a piece of stone of higher rise than adjacent stones, which is used to end a horizontal mortar joint at the point where it is set.

Keystone – The last, wedge-shaped, stone placed in the crown of an arch, regarded as binding the whole.

Lava – A general term applied to igneous rocks, such as basalt and rhyolite, that erupted from the earth by volcanic action.

Lead buttons – Lead spacers in the solid horizontal joints to support the top stones until the mortar has set.

Limestone – A sedimentary rock composed of calcium carbonate; includes many varieties.

Line level – A small spirit level that can be hung from a string line. Used as a guide for laying, accurate, horizontal courses.

Liners – Structurally sound sections of marble that are cemented to the back of marble veneer slabs to give greater strength or additional bearing surface, or to increase joint depth.

Lintel – The block of stone spanning the top of an opening such as a doorway or window; sometimes called a head.

Lunkie, hogg hole, smoot, thirl, chawl hole, cripple hole – Access points through a wall which allow the passage of livestock or the shooting of game and vermin.

Marble (scientific definition) – A metamorphic recrystallized limestone composed predominantly of crystalline grains of calcite or dolomite, or both, having interlocking or mosaic texture. Marble that contains less than 5 per cent magnesium carbonate may be termed calcite marble; from 5 to 40 per cent magnesium carbonate, magnesium or dolomite marble. These limiting values are, however, not strictly established in petrologic science and are used herein as arbitrary limits.

Masonry – Built-up construction, usually of a combination of materials set in mortar.

Metamorphism – The change or alteration in a rock caused by exterior agencies such as deep-seated heat and pressure, or intrusion of rock materials.

Mortar – A plastic mixture of cement, lime, sand and water used to bond masonry units.

Mosaic – A veneering that is generally irregular with no definite pattern. Nearly all the stone used in a mosaic pattern is irregular in shape.

Natural bed – The setting of the stone on the same plane as it was formed in the ground. This generally applies to all stratified materials.

Natural cleft – This generally pertains to stones that are formed in layers in the ground. When such stones are cleaved or separated along a natural seam, the remaining surface is referred to as a natural cleft surface.

Non-staining mortar – Mortar composed of materials that individually or collectively do not contain material that will stain, usually having a very low alkali content.

Obsidian – A glassy phase of lava.

Onyx marble – A dense, crystalline form of lime carbonate usually deposited from cold-water solutions. Generally translucent and showing a characteristic layering due to the mode of accumulation.

Onyx – So called in trade, a crystalline form, commonly micro-crystalline, of calcium carbonate usually deposited from cold-water solutions. It is generally translucent and shows a characteristic layering. The term onyx marble is technically a misnomer, as true onyx is a variety of crypto-crystalline fibrous silica (chalcedony), and is closely related in form and origin to agate.

Oolitic limestone – A calcite-cemented calcareous stone formed of shells and shell fragments, practically non-crystalline in character.

Opalized – The introduction into a rock of siliceous material in the form of opal (hydrous silicate).

Palletized – A system of stacking stone on wooden pallets. Palletized stone is easily moved and transported by modern handling equipment. Palletized stone generally arrives at the job site in better condition than un-palletized material.

Panel – A finished stone unit used on walls.

Paving – Stone used as an exterior-wearing surface, as in patios, walkways, driveways, etc.

Perrons – Slabs of stone set on other stones, serving as steps and arches in gardens.

Phenocryst – In igneous rocks, the relatively large and conspicuous crystals in a finer-grained matrix or ground mass.

Pinning, pinning stone, pinners, wedges – Small stone used for jamming at the back of face-stones to counter any movement.

Pitched stone – Stone having arris clearly defined; the face, however, is roughly cut with a pitching chisel used along the line that becomes the arris.

Plinth – The lower, square, part of the base of a column. A square base or a lower block, as of a pedestal. The base block at the juncture or baseboard, and trim around an opening.

Plucked finish – Obtained by rough-planing the surface of stone, breaking or plucking out small particles to give rough texture.

Pointing – A method of using mortar to secure joins between stones. The final filling and finishing of mortar joints that have been raked out.

Polished finish – The finest and smoothest finish available in stone, characterized by a high lustre (gloss) and strong reflection of incident light, generally only possible on hard, dense materials.

Porphyry – An igneous rock in which relatively large and conspicuous crystals (phenocrysts) are set in a matrix of finer crystals.

Processing – The work involved in transforming building stone from quarry blocks to cut or finished stone. This includes primary sawing into slabs; it may also include both hand and mechanical techniques such as sawing, drilling, grinding, honing, polishing and carving.

Projections – This refers to the pulling out of stones in a wall to give an effect of ruggedness. The amount each stone is pulled out can vary between 0.5 and 1.5in (1.3 – 3.8cm). Stones are either pulled out at the same degree at both ends, or one end is pulled out, leaving the other end flush with the majority of the veneer.

Pumice – An exceptionally cellular, glassy lava resembling a solid froth.

Quarry – The location of an operation where a natural deposit of stone is removed from the ground.

Quartz – A silicon dioxide mineral that occurs in colourless and transparent or coloured hexagonal crystals, and also in crystalline masses. One of the most common minerals, the chief constituent of sandstone.

Quartzite – A compact, granular rock composed of quartz crystals, usually so firmly cemented as to make the mass homogenous. The stone is generally quarried in stratified layers, the surfaces of which are unusually smooth. Its crushing and tensile strengths are extremely high; the colour range is wide.

Quartzitic sandstone – A sandstone with a high concentration of quartz grains and siliceous cement.

Quoins – Stone at the corner of a wall emphasized by size, projection and rustication or by a different finish.

Random walling – Undressed walling stone. Stone in its natural state. Phrase used by quarries to identify dry stone walling product.

Range – A course of any thickness that is continued across the entire face. All range courses need not be of the same thickness.

Reglet – A narrow, flat moulding of rectangular profile.

Relief or relieve – Ornament in relief. The ornament or figure can be slightly, half or greatly projected.

Retaining wall – A single-skinned wall, usually built to stop erosion on soil banks or river sides. Retaining walls can form attractive garden features around the sides of ponds and planting beds.

Return head – Stone facing with the finish appearing on both the face and the edge of the same stone, as on the corner of a building.

Reveal – The depth of stone between its outer face and a window or door set in an opening.

Ribbon – Narrow bands of rock differing to various degrees in chemical composition and colour from the main body of the slate or stone; in other words, bands.

Rift – The most pronounced direction of splitting or cleavage of stone. Rift and grain may be obscure, as in some granites, but are important in both quarrying and processing.

Rip rap – Irregularly shaped stones used for facing bridge abutments and fills; stones thrown together without order to form a foundation or sustaining walls.

Riser – The vertical face of a step.

Rock (pitch) face – Similar to split face, except that the face of the stone is pitched to a given line and plane, producing a bold appearance rather than the comparatively straight face obtained in split face.

Rock – An integral part of the earth's crust composed of an aggregate of grains of one or more minerals. (Stone is the commercial term applied to quarry products.)

Rodding – Reinforcement of a structurally unsound marble by cementing reinforcing rods into grooves or channels cut into the back of a slab.

Roman arch – Semi-circular arch.

Rough sawn – A marble surface finish accomplished by the gang-sawing process.

Rubbed finish – Mechanically rubbed for smoother finish.

Runners – Long pieces of stone.

Sandblasted – A matt-texture marble surface finish with no gloss, accomplished by exposing the surface to a steady flow of sand under pressure.

Sand-sawn finish – The surface left as the stone comes from the gang-saw; a moderately smooth, granular surface varying with the texture and grade of the stone.

Sandstone – A sedimentary rock consisting usually of quartz, cemented with silica, iron oxide or calcium carbonate. Sandstone is durable, has a very high crushing and tensile strength and a wide range of colours and textures.

Sawed edge – A clean-cut edge generally achieved by cutting with a diamond blade, gang-saw or wire saw.

Sawed face – A finish obtained from the process used in producing building stone; varies in texture from smooth to rough and coincident with the type of materials used in sawing; classified as diamond sawn, sand sawn, chat sawn and shot sawn.

Scale – Thin lamina or paper-like sheets of rock, often loose and interrupting an otherwise smooth surface on the stone.

Scoria – Irregular masses of lava resembling clinker or slag; may be cellular (vesicular), dark-coloured and heavy.

Semi-dressed stone – Stone cut on one or two sides to form an attractive face.

Semi-rubbed – A finish achieved by rubbing (by hand or machine) the rough or high spots off the surface to be used, leaving a certain amount of the natural surface along with the smoothed areas.

Serpentine – A hydrous magnesium silicate of igneous origin, generally a very dark green colour with markings of white, light green or black. Consists largely of talc, chlorite, and serpentine; further alteration may result in soapstone. One of the hardest varieties of natural building stone.

Serpentine – Marble characterized by a prominent amount of the mineral serpentine.

Shaped stone – Cut stone which has been carved, ground or otherwise processed.

Shot-sawn – A finish obtained by used steel shot in the gang-sawing process to produce random markings for a rough surface texture.

Slab – A lengthwise cut of a large quarry block of stone produced by sawing or splitting in the first milling or quarrying operation. A slab has two parallel surfaces.

Slate – A very fine-grained metamorphic rock derived from sedimentary rock shale. Characterized by an excellent parallel cleavage entirely independent of original bedding, by which cleavage the rock may be split easily into relatively thin slabs. Essential mineral constituents of slates are usually members of the mica group, commonly sericite, muscovite and paragonite; of the clay group, chiefly illite and kaolinite; and of the chlorite group. Common accessory minerals are iron oxides, calcite, quartz, and feldspar. Other minerals may be present also as minor accessories. Most slates are derived from shales.

Smooth finish – The finish produced by planer machines followed by the removal of objectionable tool marks.

Snapped edge, quarry cut or broken edge – A natural breaking of a stone either by hand or machine. The break should be at right angles to the top and bottom surfaces.

Soapstone – A massive variety of talc with a soapy or greasy feel used for hearths, washtubs, table tops, carved ornaments, chemical laboratory counter and so on, and known for its stain-proof qualities.

Sound stone – Stone which is free of cracks, fissures or other physical defects.

Spall – A stone fragment that has split or broken off. Sizes may vary from chip-size to one- and two-man stones. Spalls are primarily used for taking up large voids in rough rubble or mosaic patterns.

Splay – A bevelled or slanted surface.

Split face-stone – Stone on which the face has been broken to an approximate plane.

Split – Division of a rock by cleavage.

Splitstone finish – Obtained by sawing to accurate heights, then breaking by machine to required bed widths.

Start – A small fissure.

Stone pitching – An ancient path-laying technique.

Stone treads – Large throughs inserted through a dry stone wall to act as steps for a stone stile.

Stone – Sometimes synonymous with rock, but more properly applied to individual blocks, masses or fragments taken from their original formation or considered for commercial use.

Stratification – A structure produced by deposition of sediments in beds or layers (strata), laminae, lenses, wedges and other essentially tabular units.

Styrolite – A longitudinally streaked, columnar structure occurring in some marbles and of the same material as the marble in which it occurs.

Sub-base – Hardcore that supports the surface of a footpath.

Tablet – A small, flat slab or surface of stone, especially one bearing or intended to bear an inscription, carving or the like.

Template – A pattern for repetitive marking or fabricating operation.

Terrazzo – A type of concrete in which chips or pieces of stone, usually marble, are mixed with cement and are ground to a flat surface, exposing the chips, which take a high polish.

Thin marble – A fabricated marble unit of 2in (50mm) or less in thickness.

Through-band – The middle section of wall where the majority of stones used are throughs. The through-band ties the two faces of a wall together.

Thru stones, through stones, thrus, throughs – Large stones, which tie both sides of a wall together. Usually placed at 6ft (1.8m) intervals along a course.

Tile – A thin modular stone unit.

Tooled finish – Customarily has four, six or eight parallel, concave grooves to the inch.

Top stones, toppers, cap stone, cappers, coping stones, copeing stones, coins – The row of stones on the top of a wall.

Translucence – The light-emitting quality of certain marble varieties containing a crystal structure capable of transmitting light.

Travertine limestone – A variety of limestone that has a partly crystalline or microcrystalline texture and a porous or cellular layered structure.

Travertine – A form of limestone precipitated from groundwater as in caves or in orifices of springs (*see* limestone).

Tread – A flat stone used as the top walking surface on steps. Name given the walking surface of a step.

Trim – Stone used as decorative items only, such as sill, coping, enframements and so on, with the facing of another material.

Tuff – Cemented volcanic ash, many varieties included.

Undercut – Cut so as to present an overhanging part.

Vein cut – Cutting quarried marble or stone perpendicular to the natural bedding plane.

Veining – Coloured markings in limestone, marble, alabaster and so on.

Verde antique – A commercial marble composed chiefly of massive serpentine and capable of taking a high degree of polish. It is commonly crossed by veinlets of other minerals, chiefly carbonates of calcium and magnesium. Verde antique is not a true marble in the scientific sense, but is commonly sold as a decorative commercial marble and requires the adjective modifier verde (or verd) antique. Verde antique is commonly veined with carbonate minerals, chiefly calcite and dolomite.

Wall end, cheek end – A secure end of a dry stone wall.

Wall tie – A bounder or metal piece, which connects two skins of wall to each other or to other materials.

Walling out – A phrase used to describe the act of placing a stone on a course and not leaving enough room to work on the other side

Walling – The act of building a wall. The collective name for walling stone.

Warped walls – Generally a condition experienced only in flagging or flagstone materials; very common with flagstone materials that are taken from the ground and used in their natural state. To eliminate warping in stones, it would be necessary to further finish the material by methods such as machining, sand rubbing, honing or polishing.

Wash – A sloped area or the area water will run over.

Waxing – An expression used in the marble finishing trade to indicate the filling of natural voids with colour-blended materials.

Wear – The removal of material or impairment of surface finishing through friction or impact use.

Weathered face – The angled, front face of a walling stone. Allows rain to wash away from a wall instead of inside.

Weathering – Natural alteration by either chemical or mechanical processes due to the action of constituents of the atmosphere, surface waters, soil and other ground waters, or to temperature changes; the inclined top surface of a stone such as a coping.

Wedging – Splitting of stone by driving wedges into planes of weakness.

Wind (wined) – A twisting warp from cutting slabs in the gang-saws.

Wire saw – Method of cutting stone by passing a twisted, multi-strand wire over the stone and immersing the wire in a slurry of abrasive material.

INDEX